# OUT OF THE DEEP

## Devastated by Drugs Delivered by God

NOEL DAVIDSON

D1421677

# OUT OF THE DEEP

## Devastated by Drugs Delivered by God

NOEL DAVIDSON

# AMBASSADOR INTERNATIONAL
GREENVILLE, SOUTH CAROLINA & BELFAST, NORTHERN IRELAND

www.ambassador-international.com

# Out of the Deep
## Devastated by Drugs Delivered by God

Copyright 2012 - NOEL DAVIDSON
All rights reserved

ISBN: 978-1-62020-123-7

Printed by Bethel Solutions


**Ambassador International**
Emerald House
427 Wade Hampton Blvd
Greenville, SC 29609, USA
www.ambassador-international.com

**Ambassador Books and Media**
The Mount
2 Woodstock Link
Belfast, BT6 8DD, Northern Ireland, UK
www.ambassadormedia.co.uk


*The colophon is a trademark of Ambassador*

# Contents

## DEDICATION

David and Helen have requested that this book be dedicated to the memory of their mothers, Jeannie Johnston and Margaret Runcie, both of whom shared through many difficult days with the boys. They were aware that this story was being written but were called home to be with the Lord before it was completed.

# FOREWORD

There's a soft spot in my heart for the Broch and its people. I have a lot of friends in that part of the world. One such couple is David and Helen Runcie. The first time I enjoyed their generous hospitality was April 1999. It seems like yesterday.

I recall, before heading down to their church for the first night of a week-long mission, Helen telling me not to leave any money, or credit cards, or anything of value in my bedroom. I remember thinking to myself, 'Help! What on earth have I let myself in for? What kind of a place is this?'

Well, before the day was out, the reality hit home. I met the boys! Nice lads. Really nice lads. Sadly, however, I quickly discovered that all three of them were hooked on hard drugs. One by one they embraced the drug culture – and it showed. I saw it. I smelt it.

This book – a true story, a moving story – tells their story. Tears. Heartache. Despair. Disappointment. Elation. Delirious joy. Celebration. Gratitude. Above all, it shows in a fascinating way, the ability of God to bring the best of times from the worst of times. It says a lot about the incredible power of the gospel. It sets men free.

Today, because of grace and God, three young men are addicted to Jesus Christ!

Sam Gordon.

*Executive Director,*
*Messianic Testimony.*

# INTRODUCTION

Just before Easter 2003 I had a telephone call asking if I would be interested in writing a 'story that sounded fantastic' about a family of former drug addicts who had given their lives to the Lord and were now serving Him in different places.

People sometimes exaggerate. Words like 'fantastic' trip off the tongue so easily. On confessing to the caller that I was ever eager to hear such a story, Pastor Sam Gordon introduced me to his friends David and Helen Runcie.

I'll never forget that meeting in their home in Fraserburgh, a fishing port in the northeast of Scotland. As we sat around a table together, David and Helen told me the story of what had happened in their family. It all began with, "Well, we have three sons. David, Matthew and Jonathan…"

They were a happy family, when the boys were small, singing God's praises together to enraptured audiences. When they came into their teenage years, though, money began to disappear out of the house and the parents had their suspicions aroused. Where was it going? To buy drugs, perhaps? Could one of the boys be using drugs under their roof? Or was it just the one? Maybe there were two of them at it? Surely there couldn't be three?

As the story unfolded I found myself using that word, involuntarily. "That's fantastic!" I would whisper.

"Hold on," David or Helen would caution, with a knowing smile. "You haven't heard the half of it yet! There's more!"

There was, too. And the next episode was always more gripping than the previous one!

It was a tale worth telling, and it was only as I began to research, and then write it, that I realised the extent of the challenge I had undertaken. This is not the biography of one person, or even a couple. There are five people intertwined in this story, five people and God.

Each one of the five has had his or her physical, emotional and spiritual experiences. God dealt with each one of them in a different way. And it was my job to sort it all out and write it all down. Consider it for moment.

David the dad was a social worker. How could he cope with solving other people's problems, when none of them were as big as his own?

Helen was a mother. How did she react when one of her boys broke the house rules for the final time and had to be asked to pack up and leave the family home?

Matthew was apprehended by the police with heroin on his person and charged with possession with intent to supply.

Young David lost his job, and the new home he had hoped to buy, and became depressed, and virtually suicidal.

Jonathan was rescued from a sinking fishing boat, and then less than a year later he fell into the harbour after having taken an overdose...

Unbelievable, you say.

Fantastic?

Wait a minute, though. Where was God in all of this? Why did He not arrest these boys on the slippery slope? Why did He not appear to be answering the passionate prayers of the heart-broken parents?

What David and Helen were soon to realise, in a mighty way, was that He, who 'neither slumbers nor sleeps,' hadn't forgotten about them in their plight. And it was only when God began to intervene in everybody's life that the story became *really* fantastic...

This updated edition includes the original heartbreaking story plus its wonderful sequel.

The first edition of 'Out of the Deep' was the end product of a summer spent in close liaison with a lovely Christian family, united in the Lord and His service. My wife Liz and I now consider David and Helen as good friends and have kept in regular contact with them over the last nine years.

In that time we have heard tremendously heartening stories of how God has blessed the first book in the lives of others, seen photographs of the boys' weddings, learnt of the birth of grandchildren and followed with interest the progress of David, Matthew and Jonathan in the world of work.

As a partnership in the Lord we commend this book to you. It will prove an encouragement to many who are involved in the drugs scene, especially depressed addicts and distraught parents, not to mention frequently discouraged church teams battling to reach out into an often unresponsive community.

It contains a challenging message of hope and joy for all.

God is still in control, and He has the power to deliver people 'Out Of The Deep' of sin. Even in the twenty-first century.

All they have to do is send Him an SOS.

He never misses a call.


Noel Davidson.
September 2012.

Chapter 1

# YES, JESUS LOVES ME

The hankies were out all over the audience.

There was barely a dry eye in the building.

A sympathetic, almost sacred silence, broken only by occasional sniffling and snuffling, had descended over the congregation in the church hall in Kensalyre, a remote settlement on the Scottish island of Skye. They had been touched to the heart.

The Runcie family had just finished singing what they fondly described as their 'Love Medley,' and were returning to take their seats.

Seven year old Jonathan had opened the medley by singing, 'Jesus loves me, this I know,' in his clear, childish voice. By the time he had reached the first chorus,

'Yes, Jesus loves me,

Yes, Jesus loves me,

Yes, Jesus loves me,

The Bible tells me so,' the handbags of some of the more matronly members of the congregation had begun to click open.

Matthew, who was nine, followed with a convincing rendition of the first verse of 'Jesus, lover of my soul.' The stronger voices of David and Helen, mum and dad to the three boys clustered around them, came next in a stirring contrast. They blended together harmoniously in the lovely hymn, 'Loved with everlasting love.'

Then it was the turn of David junior. At almost twelve he was the big boy, the eldest of the bunch. He hadn't long begun to sing, 'O Love that will not let me go' until some of the outdoor men of Skye, with their sunburnt faces and soft hearts, were delving deep into the pockets of their coarsely woven Highland jackets for their hankies as well. The whole 'Love Medley' experience was proving almost too much for everyone.

When David's voice died away the beautifully orchestrated backing track led his mum and dad into the words of the challenging commitment contained in the hymn, 'My Jesus I Love Thee.' On the last line of each verse all five members of the family sang 'If ever I loved Thee,' and then the boys' voices died away leaving David and Helen to make the heartfelt, and obviously for the audience, heartrending, avowal, 'My Jesus 'tis now.'

There was a poignant interval before the chairman rose rather reticently to announce the next item on the programme. It was not that he was in any way hesitant about what was to come next, but he knew that everyone in the hall needed a moment to savour the sanctified spell that the Runcie family's Love Medley had cast over the audience. The atmosphere hung heavy with spiritual emotion.

It was in that thrilling, soul-stirring pause, with more than half of the congregation recovering their composure that young Jonathan looked across at his older brothers, Matthew and David, and smiled. It was the smile of satisfaction. A little boy's simple appreciation of what they had come to see as success. They had sung the praise of the love of God with such feeling that hearts had been melted, yet another time.

So the trip had been worth it after all. That was good, for seven or eight hours before they hadn't been so sure that it would be.

Although the Runcie boys usually enjoyed travelling around singing as a group with their parents they had begun to wonder if this outing to Skye with the Fraserburgh Gospel Male Voice Choir was going to be something different. It wasn't that they didn't enjoy the fun with the men in the bus, for they did. All the choir members, many of whom could have been the boys' grandfathers, loved the lively lads and kept them entertained with a seemingly endless succession of simple jokes and funny stories on the journey.

It wasn't the men that had been the problem on the long trip across Scotland from east to west. It was their mum.

Helen seemed unusually edgy that day. Even the slightest burst of exuberance, which could have been a laugh that was either too loud or too long, or a shriek that was two decibels too high, brought a timely warning from mum. A crumpled crisp packet dropped accidentally on the floor of the bus, or some choir member's cap chucked six seats back for fun, evoked the same response.

It could begin with, 'David, sit down and behave,' or 'Matthew, sit up and behave,' or 'Jonathan, turn round and behave,' but the opening clause of the corrective sentence wasn't the bit that mattered. It was only the opener. The punch line was still to come, and it never varied. This was invariably, "Remember we are going to stay with the minister in the manse tonight!"

After hearing this same declaration, which obviously meant so much to their mum for it was delivered with the utmost gravity repeatedly, the boys began to wonder what kind of place this was that they were going to have to spend the night. Long before they reached The Kyle of Lochalsh to cross on to the island of Skye the boys had come to imagine the minister in the manse as some sort of a mystical mix between the Monarch of the Glen and the Loch Ness monster!

The reality proved to be poles apart from their fantasies, however. Nor need Helen have worried about how her sons would cope with life in the manse.

Rev. Donald Macleod and his wife Peggy turned out to be a pair of the most warm-hearted, welcoming people one could ever wish to meet. The fact that they also had three children around the same ages as the Runcie boys helped break the ice instantly for all. Within an hour of arriving at the manse David, Matthew and Jonathan were out walking, running and playing in the grounds of what was to become their home for the night, with another David, and his sisters Aileen and Mairi. The manse overlooked the lapping waters of Loch Snizort, and the back garden opened onto the moors behind. Sheep grazed just beyond the back fence. It was an unbelievable haven for three boys from the town.

The Fraserburgh Gospel Male Voice Choir had been invited to Kensalyre to take part in the Snizort Praise Recital on Good Friday evening, 24 th March 1989, and Charlie Watt, their conductor, asked the Runcie family to accompany them as their guest group. This they had been happy to do, for David and Helen always enjoyed the fellowship with the choir members and the boys usually had a great time with them too. And everyone, from Jonathan who would soon be eight, right through to the oldest choir member who was in his eighties, shared a common love of singing. Now that the service was over, though, the three boys were anxious to return to the manse as soon as possible. They wanted to further cement the friendships that had been forged during their all-too-brief encounter in the afternoon, but they were going to have to be patient.

Their singing had been much appreciated and many adults came up to them afterwards to say so.

"That was great, boys. You are such a lovely little family.

I'm sure your parents are proud of you," one lady remarked.

"Your singing just brought me so close to the Lord," a second confessed, almost on the verge of tears again.

Although the men and women who came across to speak to the boys were lavish in their praise, the majority of the children stood farther back and regarded them with an odd kind of awe. Boys singing hymns with choirs on platforms were not commonplace around Kensalyre. The singing of hymns was even a novelty for everyone, for in the local church services the congregations sang only the Psalms. Small wonder that the Snizort Praise Recital had been such a long-awaited, and now well-attended and highly acclaimed event.

The only children who didn't keep just out of speaking distance from David, Matthew and Jonathan, when their parents were still moving around amongst the forms greeting their friends, both old and new, with genuine Christian cordiality, were the Macleods. They gabbled excitedly to the three boys about their plans for the remainder of the evening. The six children had loved the few hours they had spent getting to know one another in the afternoon. Now there was still so much to do, and say.

When mum and dad eventually managed to extricate themselves from the friendly atmosphere of the church hall, they all went back to the manse together. It had been a great evening and David and Helen allowed the boys to stay up later than usual to relax and unwind with the Mc Leod family.

Next morning the choir set off in their bus, with some of the local Christians aboard to act as hosts and tour guides, to view the rugged beauty of the Island of Skye.

The boys were happy when Peggy Macleod suggested that perhaps they 'would like to stay behind with the children.' All three of the boys welcomed Peggy's practical suggestion for a couple of reasons. For one thing they had seen enough of the inside of the bus on the journey from Fraserburgh to satisfy them until it was time to set off on the long trip back, later that day. And much more importantly, they were having a great time with their new friends.

Young Jonathan was particularly happy, however. While his parents chatted to their hosts on the bus about friends they knew and festivals they had visited, and stood gazing at the Kilt Rock and other features of interest on the island, he was having a wonderful time. His two brothers talked to David and Aileen about such sober subjects as schools and TV programmes as they explored the fields and roads around the manse at a leisurely pace. He and Mairi, who were almost the same age, roamed about together outside, dashing breathlessly from one spot to another all morning. It seemed that there was so much to see and do, and so little time in which to see and do it!

They ran for a while up over the rough grass of the moors behind the manse, with the wind tugging at their hair, ballooning out their coats, and singing in their ears. When tired of that they changed the scene completely and ended up balancing on precarious rocks by the edge of the Loch, turning over stones in rock pools, laughing gaily together as strange creatures of all shapes and sizes dived and darted for cover. They cracked open a number of shells, searching for pearls!

It was all such a thrilling, carefree experience.

The simple pursuits of that morning made a more indelible impression on seven-year old Jonathan's mind than all the singing that had so moved the audience in the recital the night before.

When parting time came that Saturday afternoon, everyone was very sad. The choir had to return to the bus after lunch to begin the long drive back to Fraserburgh. It seemed that half the residents of Kensalyre had gathered round to see them off. Rev. Donald Macleod was there, with Peggy his wife. Both of them were saying goodbye to, and shaking hands with, everybody. At the forefront of the crowd of well-wishers was little Mairi, with her hair still tousled and her cheeks aglow from a morning's non-stop exercise in the fresh, clear, island air.

Jonathan pressed his face against the window and waved to her as the bus moved off.

He had been singing 'Jesus loves me, this I know,' the previous evening.

That was good. In fact it was amazing that the Son of God should love him. But he had heard that in Sunday School since he had been about three. And he had sung dozens of times that he knew it.

But what about Mairi?

She had been his first childish contact on a one-to-one basis with a girl of a similar age from a Christian home like his own.

How did she feel about him?

Indeed, would he ever see her again?

Chapter 2
# DID YE GREET THE NICHT, JIM?

Happy memories of the trip to Skye meant that the Runcie boys had really looked forward to their next stopover engagement with the choir. And this expedition was to be twice the length of the last one! They were actually going to be staying away two nights, and what was more their trip was to include a sea crossing on their first really big boat.

It was all so exciting!

They were going to be crossing to Stornoway on the Isle of Lewis on a passenger ferry.

When they eventually reached Ullapool, the small port in the north west of Scotland from where the ferry sailed, they could barely contain their excitement. After everyone had enjoyed a meal in the Fishermen's Mission, David Runcie kept a watchful eye as his three sons explored the shores of Loch Broom.  The boys clambered in and out of the small boats pulled up on the shingle, calling to each other as they found something different of interest. Matthew played with the other two for a while then decided to create his own amusement. His game was to see how close he could creep to the dozens of seagulls down at the water's edge before they flapped their strong wings and screeched away skywards.

The bus had collected all the choir members and their wives before four o'clock in the morning in Fraserburgh that Saturday, 17 th June 1989, and they seemed to have travelled for ages through a constantly changing panorama of coastal villages, mountains and lochs, bathed in early morning sunshine. Despite the long journey the boys didn't appear to be in the slightest bit tired. They had dozed in snatches on the bus and now they were eagerly anticipating what lay ahead.

The choir had been invited to sing at yet another weekend of Christian praise. This time it was to celebrate the anniversary of the Royal National Mission to Deep Sea Fishermen in the Hebridean port of Stornoway. As had happened on so many previous occasions, David, Helen and the boys had been asked to travel with them as their 'resident' group.

Climbing the gangplank on to the Caledonian Mac Brayne ferry was a novel experience for the three young lads. This ship was bigger by far than even the biggest of the fishing boats that were sometimes jammed side by side into their home harbour at Fraserburgh. It was so spacious that they could even run around on the decks!

Having satisfied themselves that they had explored every nook and cranny on the passenger decks, the three boys joined their parents at the rail as the ship slid away from her moorings. As she sailed up the placid waters of the loch towards the open sea the choir contingent stood around in the sunshine, congratulating each other on the wonderful sunny summer weather. 'Couldn't be better!' some concluded. 'It's going to be great for the crossing!' another remarked, deriving a singular pleasure from stating the obvious.

'It's an answer to prayer,' one of the wives informed her friends, possibly anxious to introduce a spiritual element into the deliberations. 'I was a bit nervous about this sail across The Minch for my son-in-law who is a sailor over here told me it can be very rough. So I just asked God to give us calm crossings.'

When the ferry had nosed her way between the many small islands at the mouth of Loch Broom and out into the open sea the wives and mothers in the party decided that it was time for some light refreshment. Sitting down in groups where they could they opened an array of baskets and bags and produced flasks and bottles in all sizes and colours, and carefully packed boxes of biscuits. This time of refreshment and good-natured banter served to increase both the warmth of the spiritual relationship that already existed amongst the group, and the sense of spiritual expectancy that surrounded the trip.

Jonathan was glad of the can of lemonade his mum produced from the depths of her bag for him, and he was also glad to be drinking it sitting close to his old friend Jim West, (Mc Arthur). Although the three boys enjoyed the friendship of all the members of the choir, Jonathan was particularly fond of Jim who was a gentle Christian in his late seventies. They had a special bond between them.

When he reckoned that all the snack baskets were safely stowed away again, Charlie Watt had a proposition to put to the choir members. "I think we should sing a few pieces out on the deck there, lads," he suggested.

The 'lads' were all on for that. The balmy day had helped ease them into an electrifying empathy with their God and His creation and they were just exploding with His praise. It would be exhilarating to open the safety valves and express some of it in song.

As Jim rose from his seat to join the others on deck for an open-air singsong session little Jonathan looked up at him and said with an impish smile, "Now dinnae be greetin', Jim."

"I'll try and not, young Jonathan," the old man returned the smile with his response. "I'll try and not!"

In those words lay the secret of their standing joke. Jim Mc Arthur had a warm, caring heart and when he heard the Runcie family, and particularly the boys, performing some of their pieces he often tried in vain to keep back the tears. And crying was greetin' in the broad Scottish dialect of home.

As the boat ploughed steadily through the still waters towards Stornoway the members of the Fraserburgh Gospel Male Voice Choir formed themselves into a little group on the deck, and under Charlie's direction began to sing,

'Oh, it is wonderful,

It is marvellous and wonderful,

What Jesus has done for this soul of mine,

The half has never been told...'

The supporting cast of wives and children stood a few yards away nodding their heads and tapping their feet to the beat. Other passengers stirred themselves from their sun-soak on the deck and gazed across. Some even ambled over to be closer to the clustered choir on the deck.

There could be no doubt in anyone's mind that these men meant what they were singing. Jesus had certainly done something for their souls and in their lives. It radiated from their faces and reverberated in their voices.

And Jim heeded his seven-year-old friend's advice. He refrained from 'greetin'.

Instead he just sang lustily with his wispy white hair dancing in the sea breeze and his sun-reddened face shining with love for his Lord.

As they approached the Isle of Lewis, Helen was struck by the colour of the rhododendrons as she gazed ashore from the deck of the ferry. They seemed to stretch in a subtle blend of pinks and purples up every hillside as far as the eye could see. It was one of those days when to the Christian eye everything seemed to be charged with the glory and grandeur of God.

And Stornoway was waiting to welcome them!

The choir's first stop was the Mission to Deep Sea Fishermen's headquarters, just across the quay from the ferry terminal, for a meal. By this time, though, the combination of an early start, a long journey, and a hot day had begun to tell on the intrepid travellers. Jonathan fell asleep at the table when someone was saying grace and had to be carried into another room to lie down for the duration of the meal!

When the Runcie family arrived at the home of Shordag and Kendor Murray where they were to spend the next two nights they were made to feel very much at home. It was just as well, for all anyone wanted to do for a while was lie down, stretch out or fall asleep!

Later that evening, when everyone had been given a few hours to rest, the choir had their first engagement of the weekend. They sang a number of appropriate pieces in the open-air down by the harbour. The men sat facing the imposing castle, which the setting sun coloured up with a rosy glow as they sang. It seemed somehow as though heaven and earth had combined to approve their performance! And that was just the first item on an inspiring two-day programme.

On Sunday afternoon at a specially arranged service in St. Columba's Church all the members of the local lifeboat crew were presented with Bibles by the Mission to Deep Sea Fishermen. Not only did they dispense much-appreciated Bibles to the lifeboat crew but the Mission gave every member of the choir party one as well. This was, they said, in appreciation of the effort made on the part of the choir to come to Stornoway, and of the pleasure they had brought to everyone who had heard them so far. And there was, as they pointed out, 'still more to come this evening!'

Some of the choir members said they would 'treasure these gifts forever' to help remind them of a wonderful weekend. In light of that sentiment Helen felt especially blessed. For by the time they were ready to return up to Shordag and Kendor's home for tea that lovely sunny summer Sunday afternoon, she had been appointed the keeper of five treasures. All four of the men folk in her life had offloaded their Bibles onto her for safekeeping!

Possibly the most memorable meeting of the weekend was the After Church Rally on the Sunday evening. It was a beautiful evening and the choir sang outside with deep conviction, 'All That Thrills My Soul Is Jesus.' Then they went inside the church to prove, in testimony and song, that they meant it.

The church hall was packed. Extra seats had to be brought in to accommodate the people that just seemed to keep coming in a steady stream to the door.

By the time the Runcie family came to take the platform the air was hushed with an unusual anticipation. It seemed as though a Divine Presence had pervaded the place. The family ended their contribution by singing their Love Medley, just as they had done in Kensalyre. And the effect in Stornoway was exactly the same as it had been on Skye. People were moved, touched, and challenged by it.

As the choir sang piece after piece the atmosphere became so saturated with an unnatural tranquillity that in the intervals no one seemed to move or cough, or even shuffle in their seat. On a human level it was unreal. On a spiritual level it would be virtually unrepeatable.

The evening of music and praise ended with the choir singing, as they often did at the close of a service,

'We'll be there,
Praise the Lord we'll all be there!'

When they had finished and retaken their seats nobody in the packed congregation made any attempt to leave. They appeared fixed, still silent, where they sat.

David Runcie heard one of his fellow choir members whisper to another after about half a minute, "Do you think this is what it was like in the revival here on the island?"

There could be no doubt about it. Many had felt the stirrings of an element of revival during that particular gathering.

Much later on that evening, after everyone had finally left the church hall, the choir and their host families all met in the Fisherman's Mission for a supper and final farewell singsong.

While men of the choir chatted with the men of the Mission, and all the ladies helped in different ways in the serving of the supper, Jonathan seized his opportunity. He crept up behind his old friend Jim Mc Arthur where he was sitting with a cup of tea in one hand and a plate of sandwiches balanced on his knee.

When the Runcie family took part in Gospel Male Voice Choir events they were usually placed on a platform in front of the choir, and facing the audience. Hence they were never in a position to monitor the choir members' reaction to their singing.

This left Jonathan with a question on his mind. And it was one to which he was always anxious to know the answer. There was nothing for it but to ask.

"Did ye greet the nicht, Jim?" he enquired, with a mischievous twinkle in his eye.

"I fairly did, m' loon," (my boy) the older man confessed unashamedly. "I fairly did."

They had a laugh together and then Jonathan moved back round to rejoin Matthew, David, his can of Coke and his packet of crisps.

Some of the older men and their wives, particularly those with no children to see settled into bed, didn't leave the Mission premises until after midnight that Sunday. They just didn't want to go bed for they thought that when they woke up the next morning the spell would be broken. That was when they had to set off back for home.

It didn't work out like that though. The joy of the visit hadn't been in the least diluted even when the choir group reassembled on the deck of the waiting ferry to begin the voyage back to Ullapool. They had been stopping over with a number of families from the local church community and any of them who hadn't other commitments that Monday morning had escorted their guests back down to the docks.

Those already on the ship leaned over the guardrails with cameras to capture their last pictures of the crowd on the quay. The crowd on the quay, for their part, seemed determined to return the compliment, pointing their cameras up at the waving, smiling company on board the vessel.

It was a happy kind of a sad parting.

As the ferry pulled away from her berth the choir members began to sing,

'Blest be the tie that binds,
Our hearts in Christian love,
The fellowship of kindred minds
Is like to that above...'

Those of the crowd who were still standing waving on the quay and who knew the words, joined in.

The last verse of the hymn, when sung, particularly expressed the feeling of everyone, whether young or old, man or woman, on ship or ashore,

'When we asunder part,
It gives us inward pain;
But we shall still be joined in heart,
And hope to meet again...'

As the ship increased speed, and the crowd on the quay became dots in the distance, the hankies that had been used for waving goodbye found themselves employed  fulfilling a different function.

It was to wipe wet eyes.

While many hankies were still in use, a red-eyed Jim Mc Arthur considered that it was his turn to make a significant observation to his seven-year-old pal.

Finding Jonathan and Matthew standing side by side gazing longingly back at the rapidly receding land he tapped the younger of the two on the shoulder and remarked with gently mimicked childish impudence, "There's mair than me greetin' the noo, mi loon!"

And he was right.

There were.

Mony mair!

Chapter 3
# THE HEAVENS DECLARE...

Life just became busier and busier for the Runcie family. Their name and fame as a Christian singing group spread rapidly throughout the extensive Christian community in the northeast of Scotland, and as it did requests to sing at all kinds of events increased.

Soon they were out as a group two, and occasionally three nights a week.

David and Helen always counted it a privilege to sing for the Lord but the physical constraints of the constant planning, practising, and packing and unpacking of equipment could become tiresome at times. Although never tired of the work, they were often tired in it. For the three growing boys it was usually a case of rushing home from school, dashing off a homework, and changing into their matching shirts and ties to be ready for the road at six-thirty or seven.

As they set off from the front of the house Helen was often still checking that the boys were all properly groomed for the occasion and David, the dad, was hoping that he had all the equipment he needed for the backing tracks safely stowed in the boot.

There was always the temptation to ask oneself inwardly, when all the checks had been completed, 'Is this really worth it? What's the point of it all?' or 'Who really cares anyway, when all's said and sung?'

Such misgivings usually turned out to be misguided. The

reaction from the groups for whom they sang was virtually always rewarding. The response of the Young Women's Group of the Church of Scotland in Hatton, twenty miles south of Fraserburgh was typically reassuring.

It had been a busy day at work for David and he had rushed home to change and prepare for their evening appointment. Helen had embarked upon the usual routine of ensuring that both she and her sons were prepared in every way possible for their singing session for the Saviour.

Since it was a ladies' meeting David had invited two other men from the choir to join them at the church that mid-March evening also. This saved him from being the only man in the building and it allowed the three men to sing a few pieces together. Apart from these presentations by the male trio the Runcie family assumed responsibility for the remainder of the evening's programme. Some of them performed solos and duets and all five joined in singing a number of pieces with challenging themes.

Their Love Medley brought tears to the eyes as it had always done.

Many who had never heard their exultant presentation of the 'Great and Wonderful Day' were thrilled with both the sincerity of the singing and the joyful, hopeful content of the message...

"Twill be a great and wonderful day
When the redeemed of the Lord fly away.
When we hear the trumpet sound
And our feet rise from the ground,
On that great and wonderful day...

Amidst the surprise when we all arise
On that one way journey to heaven
You'll make no progression

With your worldly possessions
On that one way journey to heaven
The treasures of this earth cannot be compared
With what God for His children has prepared
On that great and wonderful day...'

Later in the evening, and after David had given a short but relevant address from the Scriptures, the family joined to ask the series of important questions contained in the lines of the hymn...
'Have you been to Jesus for the cleansing power?
Are you washed in the blood of the Lamb?
Are you fully trusting in His grace this hour?
Are you washed in the blood of the Lamb? ...'

At the supper session after the service a number of the women who had been present took the opportunity to approach various members of the group and express their appreciation. One lady said to Jonathan, "That was lovely to hear you singing Jesus Loves Me, son. I haven't heard that since my Sunday School days. It just took me back all those years."

Another spoke to his mother. "That was a marvellous song about the Great and Wonderful Day, Helen," she began. " I never heard that one before in my life. It just made me think of the Lord's coming, and heaven and being with my husband again. Forever. That will be a great and wonderful day indeed."

She then excused herself hastily. The lady, who was one of the oldest in the gathering and obviously a widow, must have felt an impending urge to weep, either from joy, or sorrow, or a strange combination of both, so she slipped away for a moment of personal reflection.

It had been a profitable evening, well worth all the hassle

of organisation and preparation. David and Helen felt that there had been a very real, almost mildly reprimanding sense of the presence of God in that meeting. It was as though their Heavenly Father was telling them that no amount of time spent, or effort expended, in His service was ever wasted.

And as they packed up their equipment and said their goodbyes, ready to head home out of Hatton, the Runcie family was completely unaware of the treat that lay ahead. They had absolutely no idea that they were to be accorded front row seats in a divinely choreographed demonstration of His heavenly splendour.

When driving northwards towards Fraserburgh David and Helen, who were in the front seats, were the first to become aware of the spectacle that had begun to unfold before them.

The sky had slowly become awash with colour.

"Look out here at the front, boys," Dad said, drawing the attention of his sons, who were sometimes apt to take a nap on the way home from a faraway function, to a light show which it was impossible to miss.

"We must get away from all the roadside lights, then we will see it so much better," he went on. Having made that observation, and with everyone else in the car too engrossed in what was going on around them to make any response, he turned off into the next minor road to the left. After driving another mile deep into the heart of the country David stopped on a hillside facing north, and switched off the car engine. It was just the kind of silent, solitary spot he had been searching for.

That vantage point gave everyone in the car an unrestricted view of the extravaganza up ahead.

The entire family sat in awesome silence for the first few minutes after stopping. The sky before them had been transformed into a veritable curtain of colour. This heavenly drape stretched from high in the night sky right down to the land horizon.

The background of the curtain seemed as though it had been painted in a soft, pale green hue, and this was laced with occasional, irregular stripes and splashes of pink and purple.

It was magnificent.

Then, as the family watched, spellbound, the curtain of colour began to move. It was as though someone had opened the door of a drawing room in an expensive modern mansion causing the delicately dyed draperies to ripple along their length in a gentle draught. Waves of brighter light gatecrashed the party every now and again, washing across the shimmering curtain from one end to another. Unexpected, startling flashes of red, purple and pink light shot like flaming spears from the top of the wafting wall of colour at intervals.

After the first few mesmerising minutes had passed with the performance still continuing, undimmed and undiminished, the family began to comment on the marvel of the spectacle. And speculate on its significance.

"This is like a fireworks display," Matthew remarked at one point, and it was an apt description. The only difference was that any fireworks display they had ever been to before had its high points and low points. There were always short lulls in the programme as the performance built up to a crescendo.

This show, though, just went on unabated.

It was all crescendo.

David junior, who was then thirteen, had remained rather pensive as the sky kept changing colour before his eyes. He had been reflecting on what they had sung so heartily back in Hatton. Then he had begun putting 'two and two together'. There was going, they believed, to be a 'great and wonderful day' when Christian's 'feet would leave the ground.' That would be when they would make their aerial ascent, their 'one way journey to heaven.'

"Could this be the Second Coming?" he asked very seriously, no doubt concerned.

"No, I don't think so, David," his dad was quick to explain. "What we are seeing here is the Aurora Borealis. The more common name for it is The Northern Lights. It only occurs in the northern parts of the country, like here, where we are now. We are very privileged tonight I can tell you. Most people have never seen it as brilliant and dazzling as this in their life times. Some never see it."

Mum had a different perspective on the non-stop light parade.

"This reminds me of a verse in the Psalms that I was reading in my Quiet Time one day last week," she told the carload of enraptured eyewitnesses. "My notes suggested that the psalmist was possibly looking up at the night sky when he wrote, 'The heavens declare the glory of God; the skies proclaim the work of his hands…'"

To her what they were being privileged to watch was nothing more, or less, than a magnificent manifestation of the might and majesty of her God.

When they began to realise that it had grown both late and cold in the car, David started up again to continue the journey home, with the Aurora Borealis still illuminating the northern sky.

Helen remained deep in thought as the spears of light just went on and on, shooting and streaking ahead of her.

No. It hadn't been the Second Coming.

But it had been a great and wonderful day. And display.

In more ways than one.

Chapter 4
# GOD'S MONEY IS MISSING

"Do you not have a tape we could buy?" the elderly lady enquired.

It was the first time she had ever heard the Runcie family sing, and she had been both inspired and impressed. She felt, too that she was speaking, not only for herself, but for the group of her friends who were queued up to shake hands with David at the end of one of the family's earliest appearances. "We would just love to take that music home with us," she went on to add, enthusiastically. "I, for one, would listen to it all day if I could!"

She wasn't the first, or the only one, to express that sentiment, either.

As their singing ministry continued to be blessed of God to a variety of people coping with an assortment of life situations, David and Helen had become increasingly inundated with requests for recordings.

With such a demand, David decided to put his skills in the use of electronic equipment to good use, and he produced the first family tape. It was called, 'Something To Sing About', and proved extremely popular with those attending the services where they sang.

When he discovered that he had seriously underestimated the apparently insatiable appetite of the general Christian public for their kind of music David produced another large batch of tapes. And then, to satisfy those who had begun to follow their approving, "We really love your tape. It just plays non-stop in the car," with the injunction, "Be sure and let us know when the next one's coming out!" the family recorded another. And another. 'Thank You Jesus' and the Christmas collection, 'Merry Christmas To You,' followed one another in quick succession.

There soon came a time when David recognised that he would have to give his recording ministry a name to provide it with a distinct identity, so RJ Tapes was set up. The formation of this organisation to record Christian music led to an increase in two different aspects of that work. One was a responsibility, the other a privilege.

The responsibility came from the steady growth in the sales of the tapes. It was the need to handle large sums of money, usually in cash.

The privilege was also two-pronged. It involved helping others through the ministry in a couple of different ways.

The first of these was the support given to Christian work and charities. When their inaugural tape began to enjoy unprecedented sales David and Helen were left with the dilemma, "What do we do with all this money? After all it isn't ours. This is **God's** money."

Since they considered that any profit on the sale of the tapes belonged to God they had no hesitation in deciding that these funds should be channelled into His work. Their initial project was to provide a much-needed overhead projector and screen for the Sunday School in their church.

This target was achieved within a year, and they then heard of other Christian singers who were interested in, and involved with, various enterprises both at home and overseas. David and Helen helped support these charities through the proceeds of R.J. Tapes.

For example an evangelical church in Spain was in urgent

need of refurbishment so funds were sent to help meet the expense of these essential repairs, and a missionary based in Switzerland had his car replaced by a slightly more reliable model. In recognition of the fact that sixty per cent of the Runcie quintet were still young schoolboys, regular donations were forwarded to Child Evangelism Fellowship to help further the work of reaching boys and girls with the Gospel.

The amazing thing was that when David, or the chairman of the event, announced that all the proceeds from the sale of the tapes on a particular evening would be forwarded to some commendable Christian cause, people bought more tapes, and gave more generously. It was common for buyers to offer a five-pound note for a couple of two-pound tapes with the instruction, "Just keep the change and put it towards that evangelical outreach you were telling us about."

The second way in which David and Helen were able to help others through the tape ministry was that David began to produce albums for a number of local Christian singers with an obvious talent for presenting the message in song, but no aspirations to make it in the big time. The whole focus of their lives was to serve and praise the Lord. He then moved on from recording solo artists to making albums for groups, Gospel choirs and Festivals of Male Voice Praise.

The featured performers in turn sold their tapes and used the money from sales to support a Christian charity of their choice. Others returned it to David to help defray his expenses or fund the current cause.

With the family kitchen often converted into a temporary recording studio and an ever-increasing turnover in tapes, David was soon handling sizeable sums of money. Since he and Helen sold not only their own family albums but also those of a number of others on their outings he operated his own rather elementary scheme for handling their own, and everyone else's tape money.

This consisted of a series of envelopes each clearly marked with the name of a singer or group. These envelopes, one of which sported the terse title, 'Ours,' were stored in a specially designated drawer in his and Helen's bedroom. When he had anything to deposit in an envelope David merely crossed out the existing figure on the front of it and replaced it with the new total. Similarly if he wanted to give anyone some or all of the contents of his or her envelope his skills in subtraction came into play. At weekends when they were often out singing twice and occasionally even three times David could have had two or three hundred pounds to allocate across his envelope collection.

It was all so simple.

In the early nineties, however, David began to question his own ability in financial management. There were times when the balances on the envelopes didn't tally with the amount of money in the envelopes when he could have sworn they should have been right.

Was he losing his ability to count?

Or was it just that he was losing his head? Becoming forgetful before he was forty?

He was soon asking himself all sorts of silly questions, or standing talking to himself with an array of envelopes spread out on the bed.

'Did I not put that money in that envelope on Friday night?' he would wonder.

'I must have given George money out of his envelope recently,' he would try to console himself, doubting all the while if he had, nonetheless.

'I was sure Sammy had more than that,' he would say, delving his hand deep into another envelope in desperation, hoping to find a ten-pound note stuck in it somehow.

'Ours' was the easiest envelope for which to find an excuse. It was always his wife, the only other person who was ever in their bedroom. 'Helen must have taken something out of it to pay somebody for something,' he would conclude, almost convinced.

As time went on, and these unexplained discrepancies kept occurring, David began to have sneaking suspicions, disturbing doubts. Although the amounts involved were usually small the disparity was always downwards. The amount of the money **in** the envelope was invariably less than the amount of money shown **on** the envelope.

Why should this be?

Surely if he had started to make mistakes he would make them the other way too, at least once. But he had never done that. Ever.

Could somebody be taking the money?

Impossible. Unthinkable. Surely not.

He shared his concerns with Helen but they decided to do nothing about it, at least for a while. Considering the options open to him he was at a loss to know what he could do. He felt he needed to keep the money in the house to be easily accessible, he wasn't Sherlock Holmes, and nobody had ever heard of surveillance cameras.

Meanwhile, and despite the constant niggling conviction that something, somewhere, wasn't quite right, David found himself spending more and more of his leisure time recording. A steady stream of new talent was coming forward, asking about the possibility of having albums made.

This pressure led him to realise, in the summer of 1993, that it was time to update both his by then fairly antiquated equipment, and the image of his organisation.

It seemed an opportune time to consider such changes, for the family had made what was to be their last tape in the spring of that year. The boys had grown older, their clear childish voices had broken, and they had begun to develop their own pattern of interests in the evenings. David was now sixteen, Matthew fourteen, and Jonathan twelve, and for some reason travelling for miles to sing with mum and dad didn't seem to appeal to them anymore.

David and Helen recognised this and so set themselves to sing together as a duet when asked, and to help others in the Christian music scene. But to achieve this second goal David definitely needed more modern recording gear.

The first move he made was to consult with his friend and colleague Peter Drysdale on how to update the image of the organisation and give it a new name. Considering that they were now dealing with more than just audiotapes the former RJ Tapes was renamed Christian Faith Ministries.

The name change, though, was the easy part.

Modernising the equipment to make it more effective, and hence the end product more acceptable in an increasingly hi-tech society, would take more time. And money.

'A thousand pounds' tripped off the tongue easily but David was sure that this enterprise was the programme that God had laid out for his life, and that He would provide the funding, in His own time, through the income of Christian Faith Ministries.

This was God's work. And God had always provided for David's needs in the recording ministry, sometimes in wonderful ways, before. It was hardly likely that He was going to change now. Indeed the Bible assured him that 'Jesus Christ' is 'the same, yesterday, today and forever.'

It was a good promise to lay hold upon, going forward.

So David printed the words CHRISTIAN FAITH MINISTRIES on a new, stiff brown envelope and introduced it to his in-the-drawer collection. This addition rendered the 'Ours' envelope temporarily redundant. Helen and David had decided that any income from the sale of the Runcie family tapes should, until the imminent need was met, be redirected into it. When news spread of David's plans for refurbishment, some of the singers and groups for whom he had made recordings told him, "Just put any pound or two you make on our tapes towards buying your new equipment, too."

That was a busy autumn of singing engagements for David and Helen and the sales of their tapes, and those of others, were unusually encouraging. The couple were quick to recognise that the Lord was doing 'exceeding abundantly above all that we can ask or even imagine,' as He always does, and the fund grew rapidly.

By January 1994 David's second column of crossed out figures revealed that there was just over six hundred pounds in the envelope. It was thrilling. If money continued to come in at this rate he would be ordering the new units he needed by the summertime. He might even be able to start looking through catalogues and talking to technicians at Easter!

Then, with everything apparently on course, something sinister happened.

The envelope containing the contributions towards the purchase of the new equipment disappeared. It just vanished without trace, melted into thin air.

David discovered it missing when he went into the bedroom to deposit the takings from the sales of tapes in it, after an evening engagement. And it wasn't there!

A weakening, sickening, sinking feeling came over him.

Where could it be?

He searched frantically through the drawer.

Perhaps it had just been misplaced.

No. It hadn't.

Perhaps he had made a mistake and put it in the *wrong* drawer.

He scurried through every drawer in the chest.

No. He hadn't.

He hurried down to the living room to ask Helen.

His wife had only to take one look at his ashen face to know there was something dreadfully amiss with her David.

Had she moved, or even seen, the Christian Faith Ministries envelope? he was desperate to find out.

No. She hadn't.

Helen then joined in the search, and in the questioning.

They both began to look in every most likely place they could think of.

As ideas came to Helen she called them out.

"Did you move it to a safer place?" she asked.

"No. I don't think I did," he answered.

"Could it be in one of your briefcases?" she enquired.

"No. I have looked in the both of them," he replied.

"Maybe it's in the car," she suggested.

"No. It's most definitely not. Why ever do you think it would be in the car?" he retorted. The tension was starting to grow. And the frustration was starting to show.

They had now both begun to look in every most unlikely place they could think of. Still no envelope.

After a sleepless night Helen had just one more proposal to make in the morning. And it hurt a mother horribly to make it. "Perhaps you should speak to the boys about it, David," she said. "One of them might know something."

That had been David's thought, exactly, but the idea that one of their lively but loveable young sons had been somehow involved in the mystical disappearance of that envelope didn't bear thinking about.

"Yes, I will do that, Helen, if it doesn't turn up," he replied.

Despite further searches the envelope didn't turn up, so father brought his three sons together that next evening and explained what had happened.

His description of the money's disappearance drew gasps of horror from them.

All three said that they knew nothing about it.

"How could we," one replied in apparent astonishment, "sure we are never in your bedroom?"

"There are dozens of people come into this house every week, your friends, and our friends," another suggested. "Maybe one of them sneaked into your bedroom and pinched it."

There were crazy ideas advanced, but all three boys maintained that they had never seen the money. They didn't even know it was there, they said.

This annoyed their father.

He had a suspicion that one, or perhaps all of them, was not telling the truth.

Feeling that a warning from the Scriptures would perhaps lead to one of them volunteering even the smallest snippet of information, David recounted, in graphic detail, the story of Ananias and Sapphira from the New Testament.

"You know boys, they were punished because they tried to rob God. And the Bible asks the question, 'Will a man rob God?' That is exactly what has happened here you know. That money that has so mysteriously vanished isn't my money. It isn't your mum's money. It is **God's** money. And God's money is missing. Somebody has robbed God under our roof."

Even this grave warning brought no response from the boys.

Eventually, exasperated, David dismissed them.

There was nothing else left for him to do.

For there was nothing else left for him to say.

His sons' blank, expressionless faces as they left the room did nothing to convince him of their professed innocence.

The fact remained. God's money was missing.

And somebody, somewhere knew where it was.

What on earth was going on?

# Chapter 5

# WHAT *WILL* THE PEOPLE THINK?

An omen that God's money had possibly begun to be used for less honourable purposes than the promotion of His kingdom came on Saturday, 2 nd April 1994. It was the Easter weekend and Easter weekends were traditionally busy weekends for the Fraserburgh Gospel Male Voice Choir. They were usually invited to sing the praises of the crucified, risen Saviour at different locations over the holiday period.

On that particular Saturday evening their engagement was in Old Meldrum and David and Helen had been asked to sing a few duets as part of the programme. It had been a pleasant refreshing evening in enthusiastic Christian company and David and Helen drove back home in as relaxed a mood as their anxious minds would ever allow them. Performing with the choir always afforded them at least a few hours of encouragement and relief. When focussing on their singing commitments they were forced to forget for a while their niggling suspicions that something both inexplicable and unwelcome was happening in their once cosy Christian home.

The initial shock for David and Helen that evening came when Ian, David's brother, came out of their house to meet them.

'What's Ian doing here at this time of night, with us not even at home?' they wondered simultaneously. To make matters worse, Ian looked worried. It was perfectly plain from his appearance that he was not the bearer of glad tidings.

"Is there something wrong, Ian?" Helen asked as soon as she stepped out of the car.

"It's Jonathan. I'm afraid he has been sick," Ian replied, pleased to have that bit over. The ice was broken, but that was merely the first instalment of the story.

"Where is he now?" his mother wanted to know. Like any caring mother she wanted to be by her son's side as soon as possible.

"He's up in bed," Ian went on to tell her, speaking softly as he followed her into the house. Then dropping his voice even lower he added, "But I'm afraid you won't get much sense out of him tonight."

"What do you mean I won't get much sense out of him tonight, Ian? What are you talking about?" Helen turned and asked as she climbed the stairs to his bedroom.

"What I mean is, he is liable to be sleeping the most of the night," her brother-in-law explained, as sensitively as he could. He was delaying the moment of truth as long as possible.

"So what's wrong with him?" his mother enquired, her voice rising involuntarily. She was becoming visibly apprehensive. By this time, however, she had reached the bedroom door so Ian chose not to volunteer any further information in the meantime.

A turn of the handle and a few steps forward would provide her with the answer to her final question.

When Helen Runcie entered her youngest son's bedroom she knew, both from the look of the boy in the bed and the awful smell, that Jonathan clearly had been, and still was, very sick. Ian had laboured hard in their absence and had cleared up the mess but an unpleasant aroma remained. It was nauseous. But Helen could cope with the smell.

It was the appearance of her son that broke her heart the moment she saw him.

This wasn't the happy, healthy, carefree thirteen-year-old she had left behind at home four or five hours before. She had been sure he would be safe in the care of his two older brothers.

As he lay there his pallid face was bathed in perspiration. He remained almost motionless. The only sign that her son was still alive at all was the flickering of his eyebrows and the occasional long moan.

"What has happened to him?" Helen asked. She had just burst into tears.

Realising that his brother was on his way up the stairs after them Ian said, "Wait until David comes up and I will tell you both together."

Within seconds David was beside them, and his first question was an almost word-for-word repeat of his wife's. "What has happened to Jonathan?" he enquired. He, too, was shocked at the look of his son.

Painfully aware that the dreaded moment of truth had now come, Ian began, "You want to know what has happened here. Let me tell you as much as I know."

He paused and looked from one worried face to the other before resuming, "Earlier this evening I was at the Youth Convention in the Assembly of God Church hall. Things were going pretty much as usual when a man who must have known who Jonathan was came in looking for me. He asked if I was Jonathan Runcie's uncle and I told him that I was. The bloke then said, 'Well I think you had better come outside here and have a look at him. He's being sick all over the place.' So I told one or two of the other leaders that I was going out for a minute and went with him."

"And is this the state you found Jonathan in?" David interrupted him. He just couldn't believe it.

"Was he on his own? Was there nobody else with him?"

his mother butted in as well. She couldn't come to terms with this situation either. It was like something you heard about in other unfortunate families. But it could never happen in hers.

"I was coming to all of that," Ian took up the story again, patiently. "Yes. This is how I found Jonathan. The only difference was he was being violently sick all the time then. And there were one or two of his friends with him, when I went out at first, but they soon made themselves scarce when I started asking a few questions."

"Well what made him so sick?" was the distraught mother's next concern.

"I asked his mates that and they said he had a bottle of cheap wine. He had boasted to them that he could drink every drop of it," Ian continued. He dropped his voice to a mere whisper before carrying on, "And apparently that's what he did."

So that was it!

That's why he had been so sick.

Jonathan was drunk.

What a discovery!

To devoted Christian parents this wasn't just a heart-rending disappointment. It felt more like a major disaster.

When David had recovered his senses after having had a brief blackout from the effects of that knockout blow he blurted out the one and only question that occurred to his befuddled brain. "But how or where would a thirteen-year-old be able to get his hands on a bottle of cheap wine in the first place?" he enquired, puzzled.

"I don't know, David," his brother replied. "To be honest I was too busy looking after Jonathan to think of asking that. Anyway, as I told you, his mates cleared off in a very short space of time after I appeared. They were obviously too scared to tell me anything more."

The realisation that Jonathan had been in possession of a bottle of wine had somehow set a series of alarm bells ringing in his dad's mind. Could there be some connection between God's missing money and his son's drunken stupor? The idea was almost too disturbing to entertain. It was clear, though, that Ian couldn't shed any light on the matter. And it was certainly **not** the time to share his suspicions with his wife. She was already struggling with a whole gamut of mixed-up emotions.

He would let it drop outwardly but allow it to gnaw away at him inwardly.

Having tried to help and console the confused parents as best he could, Ian set off for home shortly after midnight.

David and Helen were then left to cope with an agonising situation.

And they each reacted to it in a different way.

Neither of them slept at all that night.

David tossed and turned in bed trying to sort out his thoughts.

Helen made brief but pointless pilgrimages to bed, but couldn't stay.

She spent the most of the night by Jonathan's bedside, listening to his breathing, wiping his brow, praying passionately.

When Easter morning dawned bright and sunny she kept the curtains in her son's bedroom tightly closed. She didn't want to think of light, and life, and resurrection. Her world had suddenly gone black.

She spent long periods on her knees by the side of her son's bed. "Oh Lord let this be a lesson to him," she prayed earnestly, allowing her tears to flow on to the covers. " I pray that he will never want to touch this stuff again. Please heal his body and fold Him to Yourself."

When she wasn't praying for Jonathan she was talking to him, assuring him of her love, and care, and above all concern. Why had he done this? she wanted to know.

Jonathan said that he didn't know why he had done it. He couldn't explain himself.

It wasn't entirely convincing, but mother attributed his waywardness to a combination of 'bad company' and teenage bravado. There was always, she tried to convince herself, the compelling desire to be noticed and accepted by more worldly-wise companions, especially amongst boys of that age.

After a largely uneaten breakfast David spoke to Helen about the forthcoming Easter Sunday morning service. It had always been a happy family occasion before. But Helen wasn't going that day.

How could she go and sing joyful songs of a triumphant resurrection when she felt broken and defeated?

She certainly couldn't sing

'Christ the Lord is risen today,

Alleluia,' from all her heart.

She wasn't in Alleluia mood that morning.

Her husband felt he ought to go. It was important to take Matthew and David out to the service and in any event he had to play the organ. He couldn't quite think of what reason he would give to a stand-in if he weren't to turn up.

When driving two subdued sons down to the church, when sitting in the service, and even when playing glad hymns on the organ David was merely going through the motions.

His mind was miles away.

His feelings, though, were in some aspects slightly different from those of his wife.

He was as disappointed as she was. True.

He was every bit as devastated as she was. Also true.

But the difference was that his anguish was tinged with an inescapable sense of annoyance. Almost of anger.

Helen's anguish was born in love, and caused by hurt. In love that had been hurt.

David also had love which had been hurt, and that sense of somehow having been let down by someone as close to him as his own son, made him angry. He was seething inside.

This anger stemmed from a sense of injured pride.

As he sat at the organ he looked down the church occasionally at the congregation as they sang the praises of the risen Lord with earnest Easter Sunday enthusiasm.

What will all these people think when they find out about Jonathan? he wondered.

During the sermon he allowed his tortured thoughts to stray outside the walls of the church. And when he did so the prospect of further loss of face, of tarnished image, became even more humiliating.

The Runcie family were well known for their presentations of the Christian message in song all over north-eastern Scotland and beyond. And the tapes had been sold and sent all over Britain.

What will the people think when they hear of this awful disgrace?

What WILL the people think?

Chapter 6

# CHANGING PLACES

Although Jonathan's Easter escapade had caused his parents untold heart-searching, David and Helen derived some solace from the fact that the other two sons appeared to be progressing normally through their teenage years.

David junior had left school at sixteen to begin an engineering apprenticeship. That first year in the workplace dragged slowly by for the new apprentice. It wasn't that there was anything wrong with the work. He enjoyed it and seemed to have an aptitude for it. His problem was that he could barely wait for his next birthday to come around. How he longed to be seventeen so that he could learn to drive the car!

That was typical of ever so many teenage boys, and reassuring to his parents.

Matthew was doing well at school. Some of his teachers had high hopes for him academically. Parent teacher interviews about Matthew usually left David and Helen with a gentle glow of satisfaction. Perhaps he would have the ability to advance to further education, and maybe even qualify for a professional career.

It looked at one stage as though Matthew's ambitions for himself matched those of his parents as well. When asked what he 'wanted to be when he grew up' his reply was always the same.

"I would like to be a pilot," he would inform the smiling but sometimes-surprised enquirer.

An accident on a skiing holiday in February 1995 forced

him to change his cherished ambition, however. Matthew had been awaiting a bone scan because of a run of previous fractures, so when he suffered yet another broken leg on his ski-trip to Aviemore he was admitted to Raigmore Hospital in Inverness.

After being transferred to Aberdeen Royal Infirmary a series of brought-forward bone scans revealed that Matthew was in urgent need of physiotherapy. Two separate courses of treatment were recommended, one to restore his injured leg to its full function, the other to correct a curvature of the spine.

When the time came to commence his course of treatment his mum and granny Runcie would drive Matthew to his appointment. As the course went on from days into weeks, and then from weeks into months, the physiotherapists came to know Matthew quite well. They had been careful to build up a good working rapport with their patient.

In the course of a session of treatment one day a physiotherapist asked Matthew, possibly by way of initiating a conversation, "What do you hope to do when you leave school, Matthew?"

"I'd really like to be a pilot," the fifteen-year-old replied, voicing his life long ambition yet again.

This time, though, the physiotherapist's response took her young patient by surprise. It was not like anything he had heard from anyone else.

"Oh, I doubt you may forget about that, Matthew," she said, in matter of fact fashion. "With your bone condition it would be doubtful if you would ever pass a medical."

Helen and granny were both with Matthew in the treatment room on that occasion. They looked across at each other in controlled consternation. This casual comment would undoubtedly dash the hopes of the aspiring pilot in the family. How would he react to such depressing news?

On the way home that day Matthew was unusually subdued.

The bottom had been knocked out of his world.

What was there left to do now?

What the physiotherapist had predicted was probably true, there was no question about that. It just meant that Matthew would have to identify another career for himself somehow.

He sat his 'O' grade examinations in June and achieved reasonable grades despite having had his dreams for the future irreparably dented.

Although he had reached sixteen, school-leaving age, in August, his parents and teachers all combined to persuade him to return to school to commence studying for his 'Highers'. There would be, they were at pains to point out, a whole range of opportunities open to a lad of his ability with good qualifications.

He only stayed six weeks, however.

One Friday in mid-January Matthew came home from school, plonked his books down on the living-room table with exaggerated ardour. This action was patently designed as a dramatic introduction to a dramatic declaration.

"That's it!" he announced to all within earshot, "I've left school! I'm not going back!"

"And what are you going to do then, Matthew?" his mother, who was standing near him when he made stage one of his emphatic statement of intent, inquired.

"I've got a job. I'm going to sea!" her son went on to complete the picture.

"Oh no, Matthew!" was Helen's instant reaction.

Fraserburgh is famous for its fishing. It is one of Scotland's leading fishing ports. And it seems that every Fraserburgh lad has traces of sea salt in his blood.

Helen knew that only too well. Most of the men in her

family had been fishermen. But she had other ambitions for Matthew. The teachers had forecast a 'bright future' for him. The sea could be a rough, tough, man's life. It wasn't quite the bright future she had envisaged for her sons.

"Aye, I am, mum!" her son retorted. "I'm going to sea. There's plenty of money to be made at that the boys tell me. And I need plenty of money!"

"Sure you don't need money, son," his loving mum replied, piqued. "We provide you with everything you need."

"Look, mum, I've quit school. I've signed up for a three month training course for fishing. And I do need the money!" Matthew maintained before stumping off.

That was it.

No more questions were to be asked. And there were to be no more bright ideas for better jobs advanced.

The subject had been closed.

As far as Matthew was concerned it was an open and shut case. This was not how his parents saw it though. For them it merely opened another avenue of unease in their already anxious minds.

Matthew's expressed need for 'plenty of money' was just something else to worry about. When set against the backdrop of God's missing money it only helped add to, rather than allay, their suspicions.

In the midst of all these changes in the family situation David and Helen had been attempting to sell their house and move to something bigger. As the boys grew older they needed their own space. That was an understandable consideration, and one their parents were more than willing to try and fulfil.

There was another reason, which was both practical and spiritual, for their desire to move to a bigger house. It was their love of Christian people and their eagerness to entertain some of them overnight when they were visiting Fraserburgh for special Christian events.

All their initial attempts to sell their own house and buy something bigger ended in fruitless failure however. The person who had been all set to buy their house would pull out at the last minute or the house they would go to look at with high hopes that this would be 'the one,' would turn out to be unsatisfactory. It could be too large or too small, have too big a garden or too small a garden, or be too far from the shops or too close to the shops.

Nothing seemed to work.

Helen prayed on more than one occasion, "Lord, if You want us to move house, show us the house You want us to move to." She always endeavoured to resist the human temptation to add the proviso, 'And make it quick, Lord, for we are getting fed up with all this waiting!"

These futile attempts to change house lasted for almost two years until David and Helen learnt that Alex and Elizabeth, friends of theirs, were planning to move away from the town.

One afternoon Helen asked Elizabeth if she could see around her house, explaining that if she and David could manage to sell their house they would possibly be interested in buying hers.

Elizabeth told her friend that she was welcome to see around the property although she and her husband weren't planning to leave Fraserburgh just yet. That suited the would-be buyers fine. Somebody had to show an interest in theirs first before they could purchase anywhere else.

As soon as she had gone to visit Elizabeth and had seen around her home Helen became immediately obsessed with it. This was undoubtedly the very place that David and she had been looking for. The search was over!

There was no disguising the excitement in her voice as she listed all the plus points of the property she had just been to view. "It is a lovely detached bungalow in a quiet area of the town, David," she enthused. "It is big enough for all of us, with a spare bedroom for our guests. And the décor is immaculate. The colour schemes would match all our furniture, too. We wouldn't have to change a thing. There is also a lovely enclosed garden at the back. We won't find anywhere in Fraserburgh more suitable than this, David!"

What she didn't tell him was that she had already planned which son would have which room and where all their existing furniture would fit! That would be pushing it a bit too far!

Now the God who had taught His children to be patient was prepared to answer their prayers in His own time, yet again.

In September 1996 David and Helen left for a holiday in the USA and matters moved rapidly while they were away.

They arrived home to be informed by the estate agent that an offer had been submitted for their house, and if the sale went through the purchasers would like to take possession within a month!

The delighted couple then contacted Alex and Elizabeth and agreed a price for Helen's dream home. Their friends were willing to move out of the house at short notice to facilitate them and within two weeks David, Helen, David the younger, Matthew and Jonathan had moved across town, and moved in.

As they settled into their new address David and Helen began to reflect on the hectic events of the previous month and the agonising wait of the previous two years. Such musings led them to the inevitable conclusion that their Heavenly Father had so intervened in the affairs of men that their previous house wouldn't sell until the particular property He had earmarked for them became available.

God was still on the throne,

And he was looking after His own.

With all their continued concerns about the family this practical reminder of Divine power and provision brought them untold, and timely, comfort and reassurance.

Chapter 7

# TEARS ARE A LANGUAGE THAT GOD UNDERSTANDS

It was wonderful to have a new home.

There was so much more space for everybody and also more room for David's recording equipment for the still busy Christian Faith Ministries.

The family had only moved into their bungalow for about three months when Helen began to notice something peculiar. It annoyed her for she had been trying in secret, but in vain, to do something about it.

Having kept her misgivings to herself for some time she decided to share them with David one evening. They had just arrived into the hall of their new home around ten o'clock after a midweek service when she remarked, trying to appear as casual as possible, "Do you not think there is a strange smell in this house, David?"

"No. I never noticed it," came the equally casual reply. "Anyway Elizabeth would never have tolerated a smelly house. Sure she left the place spotless for us. You remember even that night when we came round here to look over the property everything was neat and tidy and everywhere was shining."

"Yes, that's true," Helen was happy to agree. "All the same I still think there is a heavy smell in here. And I don't like it!"

"Don't worry, Helen," David advised, trying to eliminate another source of concern, before it could become a subject for concern. "It's probably all in your mind. You sometimes imagine things you know!"

Helen decided that there was no point in discussing the heavy, stale smell that hung in the air, with her husband any more. He would just dismiss it as a figment of her supersensitive, hyperactive imagination. Yet despite what he said she was convinced that there *was* an unwelcome odour in their new bungalow.

David claimed to have a poor sense of smell so perhaps she should give him the benefit of the doubt. There was always the remote chance that he hadn't noticed it. Or for all she knew his unwillingness to mention the matter again may have stemmed from a gradual realisation that she had been right all along.

And although Helen didn't speak about it any further she continued to send out unmistakeable signals that the 'imagined' problem hadn't gone away. On an increasing number of occasions when David came home from work, or from being out alone in the evening, he discovered that all the windows in the bungalow had been flung wide open. This tended to happen regardless of the weather, or the time of day or night.

Helen was making a strong case. And, David had to admit eventually, and reluctantly, winning it.

Perhaps there was a strange smell in the house after all.

But if there was, what was it?

Could it have anything at all to do with another puzzling phenomenon which had begun to occur? It was the mystery of the missing cutlery.

Helen noticed that her stock of knives and teaspoons in the drawer in the kitchen had started to dwindle. She tried to blame it on her own forgetfulness at first. When she didn't have sufficient knives to set the table for Sunday lunch one week, however, she realised that they had begun to disappear. More than half the teaspoons were missing, too.

Where had they gone?

Stainless steel cutlery was supposed to last a lifetime. It hadn't just rotted away. Nor would it have been stolen. When God's money had gone missing it had made her sick, but she could half-understand why somebody could want to take money. You could always buy whatever it was that you wanted with it. Stainless steel knives and spoons wouldn't have a very high second hand value, she reckoned. And if a burglar were reduced to stealing cutlery why would he just take the knives and teaspoons and leave the forks behind? He couldn't even trade in complete sets!

No. Such speculation was just silly.

There must be some other explanation.

And there was.

The first breakthrough in solving the mystery of the missing cutlery came one afternoon when David opened a cupboard in which he kept an assortment of tools in the garage. He was looking for a special screwdriver but although he didn't find the screwdriver he made an unexpected discovery.

Two blackened teaspoons had been abandoned amongst the collection of clutter in that cupboard. He thought about it for a few minutes and then brought them in to Helen. "Those were on a shelf in the cupboard in the garage," he told her. "I wonder what they were doing out there."

Less than a week after that Helen found that one of the knives miraculously remaining in the cutlery drawer had an immovable black stain on the blade, and no matter what detergent or scrubber she used she couldn't shift it.

Was stainless steel not stainless after all?

Soon the increasingly perplexed wife and mother began to find knives and spoons in strange places. A blackened spoon turned up below an armchair in the lounge and then another knife and spoon in the garage.

It was not until she returned from choir practice one Friday evening and discovered a blackened knife by the gas hob in the kitchen, though, that Helen decided to confront the boys one by one about what was going on.

"Do you know anything about why my knives and spoons have started to disappear? Or indeed what anybody would want them for?" she would enquire of each one when she was on her own with him.

"I don't know anything about that," each one protested in turn.

"What makes you so sure that your knives and spoons are going missing anyway?" one of them went on to question his mum's allegation. "Maybe it's just your imagination, mum!" he went on to suggest.

What he didn't know was that assuming his mum to be nothing more than an airy-fairy fantasist at that time was a grave mistake!

"No! It's not my imagination!" Helen retaliated, becoming angry and utterly exasperated. "Everything is blamed on my imagination!"

Striding across the kitchen where they had been standing talking, Helen reached into a drawer and produced from it the knife with the sooty black blade. She then turned to her son and cried out in aggravated agony, "Here! Take a look at this knife! Are you going to try and tell me this is my imagination too?"

There was no response. No. Her straight-faced son knew absolutely nothing about that blackened knife or any other blackened knife or spoon or anything else.

Neither did any of the other two.

Their mother found this impenetrable wall of silence amongst the three boys as totally infuriating as their dad had done when he had gone on the trail of God's missing money.

The three boys were very close. They had been reared together, had played together, and had sung God's praise together in earlier days. Now they seemed determined to stick together through teenage. Nobody was going to grass on anybody else if they knew who it was that was pinching, and making inappropriate use of, mum's cutlery.

These persistent denials by their boys and yet their own growing premonition that they had a big problem festering all around them made life difficult for David and Helen. It was like having a boil on some tender part of one's anatomy, full of putrid pus, but not yet ready to be lanced. The temptation is always to try and forget about it and hope that it will somehow go away or become less painful. But it never does. It is ever there, hurting, irritating, frustrating.

How they wished the boil would either disappear or come to a head. At least then all the rottenness would ooze out, and the infected part could begin to heal.

Nothing as dramatic as that happened though, for weeks, then months.

Not, that is, until David was moving some boxes around in the roof space extension to make room for more incoming material for his work with Christian Faith Ministries.

It was then that he uncovered the curious, obviously home-built contraption.

He was about to lift three boxes aside when he found that a plastic bottle had been hidden down behind the pile. On picking it up David discovered that this bottle hadn't merely been discarded by some grateful drinker after a cooling drink on a hot day.

A hole had been punched through it about two inches up from the base and a tube of some sort had been inserted in the hole. Closer examination revealed that the tube was nothing more scientific or sophisticated than the barrel of a biro pen.

The inside of the bottle was all murky and smoky as though something had been burning in it. The outside of it was partially crumpled up and caved in. It looked as if someone had either heated it up, crushed it tightly or trod on it lightly.

The screw top lid had been perforated into a pattern of holes, thus completing the crude device.

David turned it over and over in his hands for more than a minute trying to get his mind around what he had just found. He thought he knew what it was. When the money had started to go missing, and then more recently with Helen and the smell she kept going on about, he had embarked upon his own series of secret investigations, as to the possible cause of such anomalies.

Just one more shred of evidence would be needed to confirm his worst fears. It wasn't long in coming or hard to find, either.

When David unscrewed the top of the bottle, the foul, stale smell that arose from that contrivance almost made him feel sick.

He replaced the cap as quickly as possible and set the bottle down.

This was the realisation of his worst nightmare. Here was the proof, the cold hard evidence that something had gone drastically wrong in his home.

What he had found in the roof space store was a homemade hash pipe.

The terrible truth was that one, or possibly some, of his sons, were smoking hash in his house. At that moment, though, he had no idea who it was, or how many of them were involved. Nor were they, if past performance was anything to go by, likely to tell him.

When he and Helen were alone in the house later that day

he showed her the hash pipe which he had stumbled upon and then hidden away somewhere else.

His wife was devastated.

"So this is where all the money has been going," she surmised, audibly. "And it would also explain the awful smell that seems to hang like a constant cloud in this house, no matter how hard I try to keep the place fresh."

"What are we going to do, David? What are we going to do, David?" Helen went on. This only served to make matters worse. It wasn't really that she wanted to *know* what to do at that particular moment. It was just that she was so shattered that she couldn't think of anything more constructive to say.

It was a good job too that she didn't expect a logical, leadership type answer from her husband, for he had no more idea what they were going to do than she had.

And there were more testing times to come.

By the autumn of 1997 the situation had deteriorated drastically.

Helen had begun to find not only home-built, but also purpose-built bought-in hash pipes in the drawers in the boys' bedrooms. They had by then become more brazen and barefaced about their behaviour, too. It wasn't long before David and Helen discovered that all three of their sons were not only smoking cannabis but they had also become cigarette smokers as well. Although they never smoked in the house when their mum and dad were present they would leave their packets of cigarettes lying around quite openly.

There was no point in trying to challenge them on the habits that were causing their helpless parents so much heartbreak either. Helen made a number of attempts.

She would find one of the lads alone, pull herself up to all of her five-foot nothing and remonstrate, "You know, son, this behaviour is not what your dad and I expect of you. We have brought you up to go to church and to honour the Lord. How do you think He feels when He sees you carrying on like this?"

"Oh mum, give us a break!" would come the dismissive retort. "Did it never dawn on you that we are working men now?"

As far as Helen was concerned that was only half true. They were all working. That was correct. David was an apprentice engineer and Jonathan had joined Matthew in becoming a fisherman, but he was only sixteen. He was still one of her little boys, as were the other two, working or not.

There was another aspect in which they could claim to be men, and that was that they looked like men. They had all grown taller than their mum and when she was hassling them about her hang-ups, as they saw it, any one of them could have pushed her over with one good shove.

None of them ever did though. They respected her too much.

They would just strut around a bit, bang a few doors and shout about not being babies any more, about over-fussy mothers, about other lads of their own age being allowed to live their own lives, and about spending their own money on whatever they liked.

The problem was, though, that it wasn't only their own money they were spending. It had come to a stage when David and Helen had to warn anyone visiting the house, or staying overnight, never to leave their purse or wallet unattended. Any money that was in it might just mysteriously disappear. There was no question about that.

Such a scenario was not only heart-rending for this highly respected set of Christian parents.

It was utterly humiliating.

David and Helen were worried, not only for the boys' physical, but also for their spiritual welfare. They were dragging their heels to go to church. All sorts of weird and wonderful excuses were offered as to why they weren't able to go.

As matters went from bad to worse David and Helen began to feel that they were losing their grip on the family. And they were losing it fast. They didn't seem to have any influence over what was going on in their own house any more.

Having sung so often,

'O what peace we often forfeit

O what needless pain we bear,

All because we do not carry

Everything to God in prayer,' they prayed earnestly, fervently, ceaselessly.

Even that didn't seem to make any difference.

There were no immediate or spectacular answers.

Despite trying to appear faithful to their all-powerful, all-knowing, all-loving God, there began to creep in the temptation to ask, 'Why is God allowing this to happen to us? Especially when we are trying to do our best to serve Him?'

Helen cried a lot.

After she had been in an eyeball-to-eyeball encounter with one of her errant sons she would often shut herself off in a room and sob silently for an hour or more. Where was all this going to end?

On one such day she was sitting at her computer typing the anguish of her soul into the machine as a kind of safety valve of expression. She was reflecting on a telephone conversation with her friend Pat the previous day. In an effort to console her Pat had been reminding her of a verse in the Psalms which says that God stores our tears in a bottle.

A CD was playing away in the background. Christian music was such an integral part of the Runcie household that there was usually a CD or tape playing somewhere.

Suddenly the words of the piece that came on arrested her attention.

It was on that subject of tears again.

'Often you've wondered why tears come into your eyes,

And burdens seem to be much more than you can bear.

But God is standing near, and He sees your falling tears,

And tears are a language that God understands,' it said.

The song was called, 'Tears Are A Language That God Understands', and the chorus was particularly comforting.

'God sees the tears of a broken-hearted soul,

He sees your tears, and He hears them when they fall.

God weeps along with them, and He takes you by the hand,

Tears are a language that God understands,' it reassured.

Helen stopped what she was doing, went over to the CD player and repeated the track. This was a totally new concept to her. When she was weeping she was speaking to God. Her tears constituted a means of communication. God understood her grief without her having to express it audibly at all.

Intrigued by this idea she decided to investigate it further. Pulling David's concordance from its place on a nearby shelf she turned to the word 'tears'.

On discovering that many of the references to 'tears' occurred in the writings of Jeremiah, she turned to the book of Jeremiah and began reading some of them. And she began to realize that what the sacred song said was true. Tears are a language that God understands. When she reached the final reference to tears in the book of Jeremiah, in chapter 31, she came upon a set of verses that she read over and over again. She was sure God had guided Jeremiah to write them specifically for her as she read,

*'Thus saith the Lord; Refrain thy voice from weeping, and thine eyes from tears: for thy work shall be rewarded, saith the Lord; and they shall come again from the land of the enemy.*

*And there is hope in thine end, saith the Lord, that thy children shall come again to their own border.' (vs. 16–17)*

What a fantastic assurance! 'Don't cry!' God seemed to be telling the distraught mother. 'Your children are going to return to their former spiritual state. They will be rescued from the land of the enemy.'

It was almost too good to be true, but God had said it and she was going to believe it.

"Thank You, Lord for this message from your Word," she breathed gratefully, reaching out for a tissue to dry her eyes.

When, though, or how, was this prophetically promised return going to be effected?

The prospect was always something to cling to in those dreadfully dark days.

There was little else.

# Chapter 8

# AT LEAST THEY'RE NOT ON THE HARD STUFF!

People often react to the same set of circumstances in an entirely different way.

Thus it was with David and Helen in relation to the crisis that had beset their home and family.

The beleaguered mother wept and prayed continually, pouring out her stricken heart to God. She also derived some solace from confiding in a number of close friends in the church fellowship, asking them to pray for the family.

Her husband on the other hand, adopted a much more introverted approach. He couldn't bear to talk to anybody about it, not even Helen. This annoyed her, for she became convinced that he didn't talk to her about it because he didn't care. She found it absolutely astonishing that he could be coming in and out of their home without even ever mentioning what was going on right below his nose.

This, in turn, merely served to add to the burden she felt compelled to bear.

As time wore on, and the situation grew worse, these completely conflicting attitudes to it began to cause tension between husband and wife.

What Helen failed to realise was that David was struggling to deal with this disturbing state of affairs in his own way.

Instead of moping around in the house, having occasional ill-natured confrontations with one or other of the boys, he stayed out as much as possible. He was a social worker and threw himself into his work with exaggerated ardour. It was ironic. David was keeping his mind totally absorbed sorting out other people's problems and in doing so he was endeavouring to forget his own.

When evening came he involved himself totally in church work, in singing and recording. And the more engagements he could take on, anywhere, or for anyone, as long as they were out of the house, the better.

He often arrived home at midnight to be greeted by the news from his wife who was in bed, but never asleep, "I found another hash pipe in Jonathan's room today, David," or "Matthew and I had a blazing row this afternoon. I don't know what I'm going to do!"

"Neither do I," her husband would grunt and climb in beside her.

David tried to sleep for he had worked so hard that he was usually dog-tired. It was difficult though, with his wife sighing, and occasionally sobbing beside him. His mind was in a whirl, but he tried to console himself that although things were in a bad state, they could be worse.

'This is only a phase the boys are going through,' he tried to convince himself. 'They are only experimenting. It will pass. This is all part of what they call 'growing up.''

Another tack was the 'it's not really as bad as it looks', argument.

'So what if they take a drink?' he would muse. 'Or smoke a cigarette or two? Or even a joint of hash? There are worse things. At least they're not on the hard stuff!'

Like Helen he was deeply concerned for the boys' physical and spiritual condition, but he couldn't bring himself to talk about it to any other person.

He did, though, pray himself to sleep most nights, sharing

the problem with God. He was trying desperately to prove the truth of Peter's advice in the Bible, 'Casting all your care upon Him, for he cares for you.'

That turned out to be a hard thing to do, though, for although he had cast all his cares on his Heavenly Carer in the early hours of the morning, when he woke up at seven o'clock they were still with him. So he nibbled at some breakfast and set off for work to try and immerse himself in another day of frenzied activity, hoping that they would somehow just dry up and blow away.

It would be great if Helen could meet him with a shining, smiling face one evening and say, 'Don't worry David. Everything's O.K. again.'

Maybe he could even find the words to express his opinions on what had been a harrowing nightmare, a fiery trial, in hindsight...

But that didn't happen.

Their holiday in July 1998 afforded David and Helen a welcome escape from the ongoing anxieties at home, however.

David had planned the trip of a lifetime for them. He organised a three-week stay in Israel, visiting many significant sites mentioned in the Bible, and of particular interest to them as Christians. They stood side by side gazing across the placid waters of Lake Galilee trying to imagine a scene on that same stretch of water almost two thousand years before. It was then that a number of terrified, tempest-tossed men, some of them experienced, but thoroughly frightened, fishermen, heard the confident command, 'Peace be still!' And there had followed an immediate flat calm.

They also sat, one other unforgettable afternoon, in the garden tomb looking silently, fixedly, across at 'the place called Calvary,' their hearts melted in adoring worship. It was there that Jesus had died for their sins. They rejoiced that through faith in a crucified, resurrected and ever-living Saviour they had both been assured of everlasting life. Nothing could shake their confidence, or dilute their joy, in that. Not even the unsettling situation unfolding at home.

That holiday was a special spiritual experience for David and Helen. During those days they found themselves drawn into a much closer relationship with God and they also felt that they would be able to sing about 'The Old Rugged Cross' with much greater conviction when they returned to their autumn and winter programme.

Having arrived back in Fraserburgh on a 'high' David and Helen were almost instantly deflated by what they found at home. Nothing had changed. The smell in the house was overpowering. There were cigarette butts in evidence all over the place. Whoever was smoking the hash had also become careless. Smoked-out pipes had just been tossed into the wheelie bin.

It was as though the smokers had become quite blasé about their activities.

The happy holidaymakers had arrived down to earth with a terrible crash.

Nor had they any idea what they were going to discover just three weeks after their return from that refreshing retreat in Israel.

It was a Thursday in late August and Helen had just arrived home from her part-time job in the local Primary School, just after two o'clock.

On that particular day all three of the boys were at home. David had joined his two younger brothers at sea, against the advice of his youth leader David Ritchie. Young David had just recently told him that he had become a Christian when still a young boy and was now trying to kick all his bad habits and live out-and-out for God. The leader had anticipated that this would probably be difficult for him in a seagoing environment, but he had gone, nonetheless.

It was unusual for the three deckhands to be ashore together as each of them was a crew-member on a different boat. Their trips often overlapped so they would seldom be at home at the same time.

Helen found that the only time she felt in any way at ease now was when all the boys were at sea. At least when they were miles out in the North Sea on fishing trawlers they couldn't be up to anything that would cause their mum and dad serious concern.

That day Helen was standing in the kitchen when her family came filing in past. Matthew was last in the line and his appearance worried her immediately.

It was quite clear that there was something seriously amiss with him.

He had a far off, distant, vacant look. His eyes were glazed and fixed forward as if they were frozen in place. He was walking unsteadily like somebody drunk. That was strange for there was no smell of alcohol off him.

"Matthew, have you taken anything?" she enquired anxiously, instantly alarmed.

"Nnnnn…o, mum, I have…n't. I have…n't…" her obviously light-headed son stammered, his voice trailing and slurring as he tried to speak. Matthew didn't stop as he tried to articulate this response but carried on out into the hallway and disappeared upstairs.

Shortly afterwards, acutely aware of an unusual, almost uncanny, silence from upstairs Helen felt compelled to investigate. She discovered Matthew in bed, apparently asleep, but she was sure that he hadn't just been tired and decided to snatch forty winks. He was out of it, totally unconscious.

The worried mother shook him, slapped his face, and

shouted in his ear. There was no response. It was frightening. What had he taken to make him like this?

His breathing was shallow, and just in case he ended up being sick Helen hauled her son onto his side. She determined to keep watching him carefully and if he became any worse she would have to summon medical help. This would be a last resort. Helen was scared to face up to a doctor's probable diagnosis of this comatose condition.

She had just arrived downstairs from one of her monitoring missions up to Matthew's bedroom when the phone rang. It was somebody whose voice Helen didn't recognise, and whose name she didn't recognise either when he gave it.

He wanted to speak to Matthew.

"I'm sorry you can't speak to him right now for he is asleep and I can't rouse him," Helen told the caller, who immediately hung up.

That was a relief. There was something sinister about that call.

Half an hour later the phone rang again.

It sounded like the same man ringing from a different location. There were now loud voices and weird music in the background.

"I really need to speak to Matthew," the gruff voice insisted. "Can you get him to the phone? I want to arrange about this evening. He is coming out for a drive with us."

"No. I told you. Matthew is out cold. I can't get him to the phone, and as far as I'm concerned he won't be going anywhere this evening!" Helen was equally adamant in her reply.

"Would you like me to come round and help you to wake him up?" was the next question from this persistent person on the line.

"No, thank you very much but I think I will be able to

manage Matthew myself," the sleeping lad's mum maintained emphatically. There was no way she was ever going to allow this individual, whoever he was, anywhere near her son, if she could help it.

Eventually the disgruntled caller rang off a second time.

It had been a long anxious afternoon and at least some of the responsibility for what was going on was lifted off Helen when David arrived home from work. She had just finished telling him all that had happened in the previous three or four hours, and he had just come down from checking on his soundly sleeping son, when the doorbell rang.

David opened the door to find a man he didn't know, but who appeared to be in his early twenties, standing on the doorstep.

His instant request was exactly the same as the one Helen had heard twice that afternoon already.

"Can I speak to Matthew?" he asked.

"No I'm sorry you can't. Matthew's not in a fit state to talk to anybody right now," David told him. How Helen was glad that he had come home before this character called!

Realizing that he wasn't going to make any more headway with Matthew's dad than he had with his mum, the guy on the step suddenly adopted a very aggressive attitude.

"You don't seem to know an awful lot about your son anyway," he sneered. "Matthew is into heroin and that's why he's lying out of it in there, but it doesn't seem to be bothering you one bit! How can you stand there so calm as if you couldn't care less?"

This audacious declaration annoyed David, and angered him all at once. He was annoyed because this man had, in one short sentence, blasted to smithereens his sole remaining source of solace in a rapidly deteriorating situation. 'At least they're not on the hard stuff,' he had kept kidding himself.

Now here was this 'creep' standing on his doorstep connecting one of his sons to heroin abuse, for the very first time.

If his allegation were true, they *were* 'on the hard stuff.'

David was angered at the stranger's cheeky, in-your-face approach, and possibly even more at his language. His derisory comments had been interspersed with a series of expletives, and this made the man from Christian Faith Ministries 'see red.' David Runcie is a big man and his immediate natural reaction was to flail out and flatten this upstart on his step. He was thankful that he managed to restrain himself, however, his Christian grace overcoming his human impetuosity.

The visitor hadn't finished yet, either. He then went on to allege that Matthew owed his young cousin money, and if David were a genuinely honest person he would pay up on his son's behalf.

When David retorted that he wouldn't be giving him, his cousin, or indeed anybody else in connection with Matthew, any money in the meantime, the man who was becoming increasingly irritated, made a most unrealistic suggestion.

"O.K. then," he went on. "That leaves me with no choice. I will have to go to the police!"

"That's a very good idea!" David replied at once, calling his bluff. "Why *don't* you go to the police? I will probably be going to see them too!"

That was it.

When the caller eventually came to recognise that he was never going to be allowed across David's front doorstep, he turned, muttered a few threats interspersed with a few more swear words, and left.

David or Helen were never to see him, or 'his cousin' again.

They were left, though, totally devastated, yet again.

They had reached another all time low.

It was after ten o'clock at night when Matthew returned to something resembling consciousness, and when he did, his mum and dad confronted him with all that had happened in the afternoon.

Although they weren't to know it that night, this was to be the first of many times when David and Helen would be forced to sit for hours with one of their boys, facing him up with the issue of drug-abuse.

It was strange, though, for although it was one of the most traumatic nights in Helen's life up until that point, she was glad of it in a way.

Now, at least, it is out in the open, she thought. Matthew didn't seem to know how to tell us what has been happening in his life but he has come clean and admitted that he was using drugs, and David is actually taking the lead in questioning him about it. And we are all sitting sobbing together. That must be some sort of progress.

There was little rest for the distressed parents later that night.

They alternated from lying in the bed trying to sleep to kneeling by the bed trying to pray.

There were big issues to be addressed.

There were important questions to be answered. They shot into their minds, and then rumbled around in them in one hazy, unintelligible morass…

How do we tell the close family?

Who should we tell?

Who can we trust?

When should we tell them?

Then there was the frightening prospect of, how much worse can this become?

And that was never to mention the more immediate, pressing dilemma.

Where on earth do we start?

Chapter 9
# I'M REALLY VERY SORRY!

They wept and prayed and made out their list.

It was their order of agony.

Both sets of grandparents would have to hear the heart-rending news first, they decided. So they made out a plan of who to inform, and when.

Then they prayed hard, gritted their teeth, and set about it.

It was such a traumatic time for everybody.

Helen was moved by the reaction of her father-in-law when he heard the news. David and Helen had invited the Runcie grandparents around to their home and when their son told them what had happened, all four of them found it deeply distressing. They endeavoured to talk the matter through but it was very difficult.

In the hall of the house, as they were parting after a sad evening, David's dad, who had been at sea all his life, and was not by any means a demonstrative man, put his arm around his daughter-in-law's shoulder.

"I'm really very sorry, Helen," he whispered into her ear. "I'm really very sorry!"

It was all he could think of saying in the circumstances, but it was all he needed to say. Those words meant so much. They bound all four people standing in that hallway into an indescribable union of grief.

That night's experience was the first of two. Helen's parents had been every bit as shattered as David's parents had been.

It was so hard for David and Helen, people who had taken such a public stance in singing for the Lord whom they both loved so dearly, to tell their nearest and dearest of their private sorrow. The most humiliating aspect of the whole affair was still to come, however. That came with the realization that everybody in Fraserburgh, Christian or otherwise, was going to hear of it soon, somehow.

They were back to the question that had never ceased to lurk in the recesses of their minds ever since Jonathan's big night out.

What would the people think?

Having undergone the agony of sharing their grief with Matthew's grandparents, David and Helen chose to refrain from mentioning the matter to anyone else until the next Sunday morning. That would be time enough.

Helen would inform their close, praying friends.

David's unenviable task would be to share it with the church committee.

Neither was looking forward to his or her role in the painful but necessary news leak. They were confident, though, that everyone in the church would be shocked to hear what they had to tell them and would be more than sympathetic. They were such a loving, caring church community.

It was David's turn to lead the service that particular Sunday morning, 23 rd August 1998, and his brother Ian, who attended another church in the town, was to be the guest speaker.

When he mounted the platform David felt his legs shaking and he had an empty, hollow, sick feeling inside.

Not sure whether he could trust his mixed-up emotions to carry him through the spiritual intensity of the opening prayer he invited Alex Cross, who just happened to be visiting from

Peterhead Baptist Church, to 'lead the congregation in prayer.'

Helen's already shattered nerves suffered an additional, and totally unexpected, jangling during Alex's prayer. Totally oblivious to the Runcie family situation, their friend Alex prayed with unmistakeable depth of feeling for 'the Christian family back in Peterhead whose son had just been sent to prison for dealing in heroin.'

The mother-in-misery just sat with her head bowed, crying silently into a tightly clutched handkerchief. A burning sword had just pierced her already broken, tender heart.

Would Matthew end up in prison?

Could that be the next act in this tragic drama?

When Ian rose to speak he announced that he had felt a compelling urge to address the congregation that morning on the words of Jeremiah chapter thirty-two and verse twenty-seven.

As he read them slowly and emphatically they flowed like soothing balm over Helen's tortured soul. If her brother-in-law were never to utter another word that morning, she felt that God had guided him to that text for her benefit.

'Behold, I am the Lord, the God of all flesh: is there anything too hard for me?' she kept repeating to herself through her tears throughout the service. Every now and then she would interrupt her Scripture repetition to launch another terse, passionate, personal prayer off to heaven.

'O God!' she would keep crying. 'O God!'

There were even more lucid moments when she doubled the length of her prayer.

It then became, 'O God help us! O God help us!"

Neither David nor Helen heard much of the message that morning. Their thoughts and prayers were elsewhere. They were trying to come to terms with their situation in their church setting. And it wasn't easy.

When the service was over everyone rose slowly, to leave in their own time, chatting with friends in the aisles as they went.

Helen was still upset, but not wishing to draw attention to herself by remaining seated when all around were standing, she rose with the rest.

Annita, one of her closest friends in the fellowship, and a confidante in earlier times of crisis, was the first to come across. She took one look at Helen's reddened eyes and then threw her arms around her in a warm hug.

"So you have found out about Matthew," she whispered.

"Yes. We just learnt on Thursday that he is using heroin," Helen replied. It was a relief to have mentioned the two words Matthew and heroin in the same sentence to someone outside the family circle. In her confusion it hadn't dawned on her that it had been Annita who had introduced the subject. Yet it had been close friends like her that Helen had come along to church that morning to tell!

"Let's sit down again for a minute, Helen," Annita suggested. "You probably won't be leaving for a bit anyway." She had heard David announce 'a short meeting of the oversight after this service,' and knew Helen usually waited behind for her husband on such occasions.

Helen thought that was a good idea, and immediately sat down again. It would help if she didn't have to mingle with too many in her present emotional state, and she felt it would be easier to pour out her heart to Annita if they were sitting together somewhere. She hoped secretly that most of the congregation would have dispersed before she started to share what was on her heart, for she knew it would be an emotive experience.

Annita had a good reason for making sure she was seated, though, for she had something even more startling to share.

"And that is all you have heard about Matthew?" Annita went on, gently probing, after Helen had resumed her seat.

"Aye, that is all I know. Is that not enough?" Helen replied, momentarily stunned.

"No. There is more to it than that, Helen." Annita leaned forward, before continuing softly, "There is something else you need to know. Unfortunately Matthew has been apprehended by the police."

"Oh no! Oh no!" Helen burst out, her thoughts reverting immediately to the people Alex had been praying for an hour or so before. She had felt an immediate affinity with that unnamed Christian family in Peterhead whose son had been imprisoned for dealing in heroin. Now she could identify with them even more meaningfully.

The sword in her heart had just been given a cruel twist.

Would Matthew end up in prison as well?

When Christine, her brother James' wife saw Annita talking in close confidence to her sister-in-law she went over to join them.

She had a confession to make. "I'm awfully sorry about Matthew, Helen," she said, her voice breaking. "You know we heard about his brush with the police when you were on holiday, but we just couldn't bring ourselves to tell you. It was so difficult."

"Oh why didn't you tell us," Helen replied, bewildered. She had now begun to wonder how many of the people she had planned to tell their awful news, already knew it.

"You came back from Israel so full of the Lord, and what you had seen, we felt it would have been a shame to spoil it for you. We realised that we were going to have to break it to you sometime if something else hadn't happened. But now at least you know…" was how Christine explained the problem they had faced on first hearing of Matthew's involvement with drugs, and the police.

It was understandable.

Meantime, the church committee had gathered in the back room to hear what David had to say. Hastily arranged meetings such as this were usually short, and often about relatively minor organisational matters, so the men assembled quite happily. As far as David knew only one of the seven men gathered there, his father, had any inkling of the gravity of what was to come.

He took a seat in a central position and began to speak, trying to control the trembling in his body, and his speech. "There are some situations that crop up in the lives of members of our church fellowship from time to time that we as leaders need to be aware of," he said, as a lead in to the news he was about to share. "I have something of that nature to share with you all. And I'm sorry to say it is to do with no other family than our own…"

He sat back in his seat, took a deep breath, and came out with it. "We have just found out that Matthew has been using heroin."

David paused, and after a couple of sympathetic sighs from his awestruck audience he went on, "As you can probably guess, Helen and I are just absolutely devastated by this. We wanted to share it with you for we will need your prayer support in the days that are to come. And also, with all this going on, I was wondering if I should take a less prominent role in the church, at least for a while…"

That was as far as he needed to go.

The prospect of David's being less involved in leadership in the fellowship had been greeted by a firm, "No indeed," from one of the men and a definite shaking of the head from the others. They reckoned that he needed to be nearer to them, so that they could show him all the love and support possible at such a critical period in his life, rather than farther away and isolated.

A shocked, stunned silence followed David's announcement of such disturbing news. Tears welled up in the eyes of big strong men who hadn't wept in public for years. Someone prayed a short, heartfelt prayer for the family, and then two or three of the men stood up. They were in a quandary. They wanted to stay and show their love and sympathy with David in his difficulty, but what was the point in staying when you didn't know what to say? When your brain had suddenly gone dead and your voice box had seized up?

One by one they began to file out, and as they did so they each one shook David's hand heartily. David knew these men well. He had grown up with some of them, and had worked with them in the church for years. He could sense the warmth of feeling in those strong hands. Those men didn't need to say anything. Their hearts were in their handshakes.

The only man to find his power of speech returning before he left the room was John Donn, one of the last to leave. "We are one hundred per cent behind you, David," he said, expressing in words what the handshakes of the others had expressed in warmth.

And it was all David needed to know. It was so comforting to have godly, sensible men like these with him and around him at such a time. They would pray for Helen and him, and for the boys, day and night from now on. He was sure of that.

They went home after that service still heartbroken, but encouraged by the sympathetic and wholehearted support of which they had been assured by the church fellowship. Their only hope in such dark days was in God, and their only earthly comfort was in the friendship of His people.

Later that Sunday evening David and Helen invited Ian, David's brother who had been the speaker at their morning service, and his wife Gail round to their home for a chat. Helen wanted to thank Ian for the message from Jeremiah thirty-two. It had been such a consolation to reflect on the fact that no matter how gloomy the prospects seemed to be, there was nothing too hard for the Lord.

They had been sitting chatting casually for a while when Helen asked Ian and Gail, "Have you heard anything about our family?"

"No, we haven't," Ian replied at once. "But I thought there must be some problem with somebody. You were obviously very upset this morning, Helen."

"Well we just wanted you to know that we found out a few days ago that Matthew has been using heroin," Helen responded to Ian's remark, giving the reason for her 'upset' appearance. "But we thought you must have known when you preached from that text this morning. We have been thinking about it and talking about it all day."

"No, I had no idea what was wrong," Ian repeated. "It must have been the Lord laid that message on my mind, especially for the pair of you." He felt humbled that God should use him to convey His word to a Christian couple in a crisis, and particularly when the couple were his brother and sister in-law.

Then, acutely aware of their ongoing heartache he went on, "We are really very sorry to hear about Matthew. We will be remembering you all in prayer. And please don't hesitate to contact us if there is anything at all we can do."

Having told Ian and Gail there was only one more family member left to contact. That was Helen's other brother John and his wife Patricia. They weren't at home that night and so Helen went to see them personally on the Monday evening.

As soon as she had entered their home John sensed that Helen had a burden on her mind. He knew his sister well. She wasn't her usual, happy, cheery self.

"What's the matter, Helen?" he enquired at the earliest opportunity.

"It's Matthew," the response came as though the floodgates of some mighty dam had been breached. "It's Matthew. We have just realised that he has been using heroin for a while, and now he has been apprehended by the police!"

Like so many others over that traumatic weekend of revelation and declaration, John couldn't think of anything very clever or controlled to say. He just put his arms around his sister and repeated the words Helen had already heard more than once over the previous four days and nights, "I'm really very sorry! I'm really very sorry!"

Helen felt a sense of calm come over her as she walked home later that evening.. She became unusually conscious that God was in control. And there was the overwhelming realization that Christian people genuinely cared.

She felt enclosed in a cocoon of their love and prayers.

They were openly, and honestly, 'really very sorry.'

# Chapter 10

# OUT COLD, IN THE COLD

At least now it was all out in the open.

As the chill of autumn gave way to the biting cold of winter in the northeast of Scotland, David and Helen were surrounded by the love and prayers of many caring Christian people. They were so grateful for this, for those were difficult days.

Young David appeared to be living a fairly respectable life, but Matthew and Jonathan had chosen to hang around with a bunch of lads who would not have been high up on their parents' list of choice friends for their family. There were times when Helen found it difficult not to chase these 'mates' from her house and tell them not to come back. She refrained from this, however, reminding herself often that theirs was supposed to be a Christian home. And was Christ himself not described correctly but scathingly by the Pharisees as a 'friend of publicans and sinners?'

It was Matthew and Jonathan too, who were involved in the Saturday night scene in the snow.

The boats had all been tied up in the harbour for days during January 1999 because of prolonged bad weather, and so all three sons were at home. This increased tension levels for everyone.

The two younger boys had gone out together that Saturday evening but when Matthew came home alone after midnight Helen became really worried. David and she had tried to be tolerant of the outrageous times their sons often returned at during the week, but had endeavoured to impose a strict rule on Saturday nights, leading on into Sunday mornings. As far as they were concerned when midnight came it was the Lord's Day and they expected everyone to be home by then.

When she realised that Matthew was in but that Jonathan hadn't yet appeared Helen became rather worried.

It was blowing a blizzard outside. Every time she rose to pull back the bedroom curtains all she could see were huge flakes of snow being driven along horizontally in the stiff wind.

Where was her youngest boy?

David was anxious, too, but he vented his concern and frustration in an outburst of bad temper.

Helen was growing increasingly distressed and that was annoying him.

Jonathan had broken the house rules and that was angering him.

"Well that's it! I'm going to sort this thing out once and for all!" he declared with grim determination, jumping up out of bed. This sudden exclamation only served to increase, rather than allay his wife's fears.

'What is he going to do now?' she wondered as she saw him struggle into some clothes.

Her husband was obviously intending to go somewhere, and soon. Where, though, could he go on a night like that?

Was he planning to go out and search for Jonathan?

What would he say, or maybe even worse, do, to him if he found him, the way he was feeling?

What will happen if…?'

It didn't bear thinking about.

David called, "I'm away!" and strode out of the bedroom, leaving his wife to her thoughts, and fears, and panic prayers.

His first port of call was Matthew's bedroom. "Have you any idea where Jonathan is tonight, Matthew?" he burst out after bursting in.

"Yes, I think I know where he might be," Matthew replied.

"Will you come with me and show me then? He should have been home long ago!" David went on.

"You mean you are going out to look for him on a night like that..." Matthew began to object.

"Yes! I do mean I am going out to look for him on a night like that!" his dad interrupted him. "Now are you coming to help me or not?"

"O.K. I'll come with you," Matthew agreed. His dad was clearly quite agitated. It would be patently unwise to protest any further.

With that father and son pulled on their heaviest jackets and set off out into the blinding snow.

The blizzard hadn't abated a bit.

Driving was a nightmare. The snowflakes bombarding the windscreen had an almost hypnotic effect on both driver and passenger. There was no conversation. David drove on doggedly down towards the harbour.

Eventually Matthew pointed to a dingy looking house with a light shining out through some tattered curtains. "That's the place," he said. "Jonathan will probably be in there. I'll go in and see."

The car had barely slithered to a stop before he had jumped out and was on his way up to the door. Better that he go and ask for Jonathan than his dad, he reckoned.

Matthew knocked at the door, and after exchanging a few words with whoever came to answer it, disappeared into the house.

In two minutes he was back out again.

He jumped into the passenger seat of the car and said,

"Jonathan's in there O.K." He hesitated for a minute, before going on, not particularly anticipating his dad's reaction to his next item of information, "But I'm afraid he's not in a fit state to come out," he went on.

"He'll come out for me!" was David's immediate response as he opened his door and launched himself out into the snow.

He banged on the door and when a man came to answer it David realised that he had been on drink, or drugs, or something not conducive to clarity of thought. He had a faraway, distant, spaced-out look.

"I'm Jonathan Runcie's dad," David began, in a curt introduction. "Is he in here?"

"Aye, he is," the man at the door replied.

"Well can I see him?" his dad went on, advancing into the dimly lit dwelling.

"Aye, I suppose you can," the out-of-it individual went on. His response was totally superfluous, however, for by the time he had struggled out with it David had already seen his son.

And what a shocking sight it was!

Jonathan was stretched out cold on the floor, totally motionless. His long hair partly concealed his grey face. Scraps of tinfoil littered the floor around him. Two empty wine bottles shared a stained settee with another not even semi-lucid character.

The air stank with stale cigarette smoke and all the other fetid follow-ups to the night's activity.

David was still seething inside. He had been forced to rise from his warm bed and then drive through the snow to this disgusting dive.

That was infuriating.

The Christian father's quest had led him to discover his son in a senseless, stupefied state on the filthy floor of a drugs den.

That was humiliating.

He leaned down and shouted into Jonathan's ear.

There was no response.

He then tapped him sharply on both cheeks, with both hands.

There was still no response.

Growing even more irritated he took his son's head and shook it from side to side.

Still nothing happened. When he let the groggy, wobbly head go again it just clonked to the floor. The pathetic looking lad remained out for the count.

Becoming more frantic in his frustration David grabbed him by the long hair with one hand and the back of the neck of his sweater with the other, and yanked him to his feet.

Jonathan wasn't able to stand. He was about to collapse to the floor again when his unflinching father began propelling him forward. It was a case of holding him up and half-carrying half-pushing him through the debris of the den to the door.

On stepping outside into the wild winter's night, the weather conditions added yet another hazard to an already perilous expedition. Father had to navigate his insensate son and himself through a swirling snowstorm to the car. By dint of sheer determination David eventually managed to frog-march Jonathan to the side of the waiting vehicle, which was by then just an outline lump in the falling snow.

He shouted to Matthew to open the back door and when one son duly complied with this command their father unceremoniously shoved another into the back seat.

It was time to set off for home. David was about to bring his disobedient, defiant wanderer back. Surely this would teach him a lesson. Surely he would obey the simple curfew in future. Surely… or so he thought.

Progress was slow. Conditions had deteriorated, even from the outward journey.

They were almost home when the boy in the back seat

began to stir. He had been out cold, but the extreme cold of the night was beginning to bring him back to his senses.

"Where am I?" he enquired groggily, trying to lift his scruffy head. "What are you doing?"

"You are in my car and I am taking you home where you should have been hours ago," David replied through gritted teeth. Driving required every ounce of his concentration and he had no desire to initiate a confrontation with his recalcitrant son in such a situation.

As it turned out, though, he was left with little choice in the matter.

"You have no right to do this to me! " Jonathan suddenly began to shout. "I'm not a baby any more! I am a working man now and I will go out when I like and come in when I like!"

"No. That's where you are wrong, Jonathan," his dad retorted, trying desperately to sound controlled. "As long as you are under our roof we will set the time that you have to be in for. And if you don't agree with that you can find yourself somewhere else to live!"

It was a risky ultimatum to advance, and Jonathan immediately took him up on it.

"O.K! Let me out! I'm going to find myself somewhere else to live right now. I don't want to go back with you. I am fed up being treated like a schoolboy!" Jonathan retaliated angrily. "Stop the car! Let me out! Now!"

David, the dad, did as he was told.

He stopped the car beside a big open park just about five minutes walk from their home.

"Don't be silly, Jonathan," he turned round to counsel, still struggling to keep his cool. "You can't go out in that blizzard. And you certainly can't find somewhere to live at this time of the morning!"

It was all to no avail.

"I'm getting out!" his son insisted, fumbling to open the

door and then stumbling out into the snow. He took one unsteady step backwards to close the door with a resounding thump before disappearing into the blizzard. It was still snowing steadily and there was no shelter whatsoever in the direction he had gone.

David put his head down on his folded hands across the steering wheel.

What on earth have I done? he began to think. Or what on earth can I do now?

He was thankful that he didn't have to do anything. Help was at hand.

Matthew, who had been the silent observer of the night's unfolding events, solved his dad's dilemma. He knew from experience exactly how rotten Jonathan would be feeling and just how vulnerable he would be.

"You can't just leave him out there, dad! He'll die out there!" he contended when he realized that his father was in a quandary to know what to do next. "I'll go out after him and talk to him. I'll bring him home if I can."

Recognising that there was no time to waste he too opened the car door and disappeared in pursuit of his brother. The snow had been a problem in so many ways that night but it now proved a blessing. Matthew was able to follow Jonathan's rapidly filling up footprints.

Meanwhile David started up the car and returned slowly to the house, hoping that the boys would have made it before he did.

They hadn't.

As soon as Helen heard his key in the lock she came to meet him. It had been a long, anxious wait.

"Where are they?" she asked bewildered, when David arrived into the hall alone.

"They're coming," he replied, with more hope than conviction.

Her husband had gone out aggressively with one son in tow, to start and search for another. Now he had come back meekly, almost apologetically, with neither.

"What has happened, David? Is Jonathan all right? Did you find him?" The questions tumbled out in quick succession. Helen was nearly hysterical by this time.

"Yes, I found him and Matthew is with him now," David began to explain, shedding his outer layers of clothing. He then went on to detail all that had happened since he and Matthew had left the house, and was coming near an end of it when the door opened.

David and Helen both rushed into the hall and on doing so they were confronted with a pair of shivering snowmen.

Matthew had brought Jonathan home.

What a relief!

The whole family was safe under the one roof.

Tensions were immediately eased.

Everyone could relax again.

Until the next morning, that was.

## 11
## NEARER MY GOD TO THEE

David continued to throw himself unstintingly into his work, both in his everyday employment as a social worker and his evening and weekend activities in Christian service, as spring approached. He refused to spare either mind or body any effort or exercise in an all-out attempt to prevent the ongoing abnormalities at home from impinging on what he considered to be a 'normal Christian life.'

Anything that kept him busy and out of the house was considered an acceptable, even desirable, activity. And it was while visiting the local Leisure Centre on another mission entirely that David had an idea. It was for something big, something Christian, and something that would involve endless administration. So it would be a totally absorbing occupation.

His partner in Christian Faith Ministries, Peter Drysdale, and he had called in at the Centre, the largest public facility in the town, to explore the possibility of using a minor hall as a venue for an event in which they were planning to be involved. When they were there they discovered that the main hall in the facility had been seated for a pop concert that was due to be staged the next day.

The arena appeared extremely spacious and had a huge seating capacity. The thought suddenly dawned on him. This would be an ideal venue for a big Gospel music get-together.

David shared his vision with Peter and he was all for it from the start. He thought it would be a wonderful idea, and began at once to compile a provisional list of possible performers. At one point in their discussions Peter remarked, "You know, David, if we ever thought of putting on a function like that it would take up every minute of our spare time for months."

"I know that, Peter," his friend replied, "but I think we could do it. It would be great to organise and publicise something positive in the town. We have had so much bad media publicity recently because of our awful drugs problem."

The prospect of unending, intensive involvement in something which could ultimately be used to help Christian people praise God and encourage one another pleased him no end. It could also have other peripheral, personal benefits for a father in his situation.

Buoyed up by Peter's positive reaction David went home, and at the first opportunity remarked almost casually to Helen, "I was in the leisure centre tonight with Peter as you know, and I thought that the main hall down there would be a great place to hold a big Christian music night or even a weekend. Peter and I discussed it and he thinks it would be a good idea. What do you think, Helen?"

"You're off your head, David, that's what I think!" was his wife's immediate and candid response. She had always considered it part of her role in their marriage to introduce an element of reality into some of her husband's hare-brained, highfalutin ideas. "At the rate you are working these days when do you think you would ever get the time to organise something like that? Whatever will you dream up next?"

In spite of Helen's deep reservations about her husband's desire to embark upon yet another time-consuming organisational enterprise, his vision gradually materialised. A committee was formed with David as its chairman, and the first National Gospel Music Convention was arranged to be held in the Fraserburgh Leisure Centre on the May Bank Holiday weekend, 1999.

The response of the invited artists, and from the Gospel music-loving public in general, far exceeded the organisers' expectations. Groups from England, Scotland, and Ireland, plus others from places as different, and as far away as the Faeroe Islands and the USA, all expressed an eagerness to take part in this initial venture.

In the midst of all the flurry of final preparations in the days leading up to the convention there were two dark shadows falling across David Runcie's crowded pathway. The first was the ever-present agony over his sons, especially Matthew and Jonathan, and their drug-taking escapades. The other was the more recent awareness of a rapid decline in his father's health over the previous few months.

The attendances at the Christian Music Convention on Friday 30 th April had been encouraging and an even bigger crowd was expected at the main event the next evening.

On the Saturday morning, and with plans for the day well advanced, David took an hour off to go up and see his father. The old man was weak and frail. He had been suffering from pulmonary emphysema for years and the effects of the disease were more evident that morning than David had ever noticed before. Breathing had obviously become a major effort for his dad.

As he left his parents' home to drive down to the Leisure Centre and be sucked into another eddy of action, David was forced to recognise an unpleasant reality. It was that it was highly unlikely that his father would ever be out at a meeting again. And he loved meetings. They were his primary interest in life. He had been so looking forward to this weekend of Christian praise, but now he would not be well enough to be out.

David talked to God as he drove down through the town. This intimate conversation with his Heavenly Father was more an observation than a prayer, more a reflection than a request. "Lord, my dad is not cut out for being confined to the house, weak and ill. He just loves being out in the company of other Christians," he mused. "So Lord, if he can't make it out to the meetings it would be much better if You would just take him home to heaven."

When he arrived down at the Christian Music Convention David became totally absorbed in his responsibilities for the day, and tried to forget about his ailing dad, at least for the moment.

The evening concert, which was scheduled to run for almost five hours, attracted a capacity crowd. Almost one thousand four hundred people crammed into the main hall for that evening event. The popular country music singer, George Hamilton IV had agreed to act as compere and David's role when the concert began was to assist the sound engineer and run the front-of-house sound for the artists.

Shortly after ten o'clock, with the function in full swing, David felt a tap on his shoulder. He was seated at a console facing the stage and with his back to the audience, and so he hadn't seen whoever it was who had tapped him, approach him. And he certainly couldn't have heard anyone come near him for the hall was reverberating to the beat of a country Gospel music number at the time.

Assuming that it was merely someone with a message about a change in the programme or some other relatively trifling administrative detail David turned around rather indifferently.

He was surprised then to look up and see his brother Ian standing there.

Without any preamble Ian leaned forward and whispered

loudly enough to make himself heard, "Dad has passed away."

David was shocked and stunned. He felt temporarily paralysed, unable to speak or move. What a blow! And what an astounding response to his mid-morning meditations! He had expected God to just somehow file away his reflections in the vaults of heaven, but not to act on them quite so soon!

On recovering his ability to communicate, David signalled to one of his assistants to take over from him at the sound desk, and rose to follow Ian from the hall.

Meanwhile Helen, who had been seated farther back in the arena, had seen Ian walk forward and tap her husband on the shoulder, and when the two brothers began making their exit she also rose, almost instinctively, from her seat. There was definitely something wrong.

When one of the American singers, Tim Lovelace, saw the Runcie trio head towards the exit, he went out another door and caught up with them in the car park.

On hearing the news of David's father's death he put his arms around David and Helen, just before they stepped into their car, and prayed with them.

It was so comforting.

As he spoke to his grieving mother later that evening, David, although vexed at his dad's unexpected passing, had a strange peace about his sudden transition to glory. His father had been out at church the previous Sunday, but had been vexed to be missing the Gospel Music Convention. Now God had called him away to a much more comprehensive heavenly convention, where the participating congregation was the saints of all ages and the theme chorus was, 'Worthy, worthy is the Lamb.'

Next day though, it came in on him. Having been unable to go out to any church services on the Sunday morning, David determined to attend the final meeting of the Gospel Music

Convention on the Sunday evening. He was in the shower in preparation for going out when he began to weep. He had kept a stiff upper lip for so long but the build up of grief craved outward expression for release. Another emotional safety valve had been released.

David and Helen found it most reassuring to sit as part of the audience that Sunday evening and listen as one group after another sang the praise of their Saviour, His life, His love and His abiding presence and peace.

They both sat and wept unashamedly as the Faeroese choir sang 'Nearer My God To Thee' with deep feeling.

It was the last verse that they found particularly comforting in their current bereavement. As the choir sang,

'Or if on joyful wing
Cleaving the sky,
Sun, moon, and stars forgot,
Upward I fly,
Still all my song shall be,
Nearer my God to Thee...'

they thought on a blissful, tearless, coming day when they would be reunited with David's dad in heaven.

With the first Gospel Music convention over successfully, and requests already flooding in for a similar weekend the next year, David had to turn his mind to more immediate matters. His dad's funeral had been arranged for later that week.

Rev. Eric Stewart from the Independent Methodist Church in Coleraine, Northern Ireland, a close friend of the family, had been invited to conduct the service.

Burying a loved one can be a traumatic experience under normal circumstances but David and Helen had an added burden that day. They had to endeavour to have their three sons, who had been operating to their own agenda for some time, at home, at the proper time, and acceptably presented for a funeral.

Their mother was back to the stage of laying out clothes. It reminded her of earlier, happier, singing together days as a family.

"Here, Matthew, that's your white shirt," she said, pointing. "And that's yours, Jonathan. I have three black ties here, one for each of you. And make sure you all wear your black shoes." It was a trial, for all three boys hadn't worn what they considered fuddy-duddy formal clothes for some time.

Dressing the boys turned out to be merely the minor challenge of the day of the funeral, however. An even greater one was to come, from a totally unexpected source.

David's mum, Rev. Eric Stewart and his wife Yvonne, Ian and Gail, and a number of other close friends had assembled in David and Helen's home for a cup of tea before setting off together down to the church for the funeral service.

Half an hour before they were due to leave, David's mum came to him. She was visibly upset. The shock of losing her husband had been harrowing enough. Now she had something else distressing to report.

"I had quite a bit of money in my handbag to meet the funeral expenses there this morning, David," she said. "I hung my bag over the back of a chair in the kitchen when I came in. Now the money's gone!"

David turned pale. Not for the first time in his life he felt a sinking feeling give way to an angry one.

"Are you sure, mum?" he stammered, incredulously. "Can you be completely sure you had the money here today?"

"Yes, David, I'm sure," his mother replied, utterly confident. "I counted it into the purse in my bag this morning."

This was sickening.

God's money had gone missing, and although he had

never managed to prove it, he was sure that somehow the boys were to blame.

Surely, though, they wouldn't stoop so low as to rob their grieving granny on the day of their granddad's funeral. It was unthinkable. They couldn't possibly be *that* desperate for money.

He would have to ask them anyway. If money had disappeared the finger of suspicion pointed stiffly in their direction.

David hustled his three sons into a bedroom away from all the others. They were looking smarter than he had seen them for months, but perhaps they held a secret.

There was little time to waste so David told them what had happened. Quite a sizeable sum of money had gone missing from granny's purse. Did any of them know anything about it?

Immediate emphatic denials by the sons were followed by the threat of drastic action on the part of the dad. "All right!" he said. " I need you to prove it to me! Turn out your pockets all of you, or I will search you one by one!"

This fierce ultimatum brought instant results. The lads could see that their dad was in no mood to be trifled with.

The money was produced, and David returned it to his mother, who in turn replaced it in her handbag.

It was now time to leave for the church.

David felt a sense of gloom envelop him as they drove away from the house.

He thought again of the hymn that had brought so much solace to Helen and he when the Faeroese choir had sung it on Sunday night. There was another verse to it which described exactly how David felt. It said,

'Though, like the wanderer,
The sun gone down,
Darkness be over me,

My rest a stone,
Still in my dreams I'd be,
Nearer my God to Thee…'

There had been many emotional sunsets in David's life, and a lot of dark days in the past five or six years.

Today, having actually proved that one of his sons had attempted to steal money from his mother in the midst of all the sorrow surrounding his father's funeral, had to be one of the worst of them.

His only hope of emotional and spiritual survival was in the assurance that God knew. And understood.

He would try to keep near to God.

Chapter 12
# THE SOLID ROCK CAFÉ

"Excuse me, Your Honour, can I speak?" the stranger in the court enquired, rising to his feet.

"Who is this man?" the judge enquired of the sheriff-clerk in Banff, a small town twenty-four miles west of Fraserburgh. It was unusual for someone to appear so bold as to address him other than in the course of the court business.

"This is the father of the accused, Mr. Runcie, Your Honour," the clerk replied.

It had been an embarrassing enough experience for him to have to accompany his son to court on a drugs charge, but the prospect of having the case postponed yet again proved just too much for David to take. They had been before and the case had been adjourned because a couple of unwilling witnesses had failed to turn up. He found the prospect of a second adjournment unthinkable. Why should he and his son, who was prepared to plead guilty, be penalised because an 'essential' witness had ignored the summons to attend? The court had been informed, for the second time, that he was 'at sea.'

"Yes, you may, briefly," the judge conceded. "What is it that you want to say?"

"Please could this matter be dealt with today, Your Honour?" was the father's request. "The last time this case was postponed my son missed a trip to sea, and I took a day off work. Matthew has taken another week off the sea just to come here today and I have had to ask my employers for a second day off. Although my son is not legally represented he is pleading guilty to the charge of possession of a class A drug, namely heroin."

The judge gave the matter some serious consideration, and appreciating the difficulties a further adjournment would create, he agreed to David's request.

He imposed a four hundred pound fine.

Matthew Runcie had appeared in his first court case and was convicted. As the judge rose to leave the court he looked down at the nineteen-year-old sternly and said, "You could have had a custodial sentence. Consider this a solemn warning. I never want to see you here again!"

A few weeks after Matthew's court case David and his friend Peter Drysdale were approached by Acting Chief Inspector Jim Urquhart of the local police force.

Jim was a Christian and he had a burden on his mind.

"I have been making enquiries around the town for some time," he began by telling the two men who were initially surprised to have been contacted by such a high-ranking officer in the Fraserburgh Police Station. "My aim was to find out who would be the best person or people to speak to in relation to doing something about the escalating problem we have with drugs here in the local community."

He paused, smiled, and continued, "The trail ends here. A number of the people I contacted advised me to get in touch with David Runcie and Peter Drysdale. They are the 'movers and shakers' in this town!

You will be interested to know what has put this idea into my head," the senior policeman went on. "So let me fill you in on a bit of the background. In March of this year I was called out to a drugs related death in the town. It was a Sunday evening and as I drove back to the station with a heavy heart at the tragic loss of another young life, I passed a number of churches. The lights were on in all of them but the doors were closed. I could just imagine the congregation singing, 'Rescue the perishing, care for the dying,' with great gusto, and then settling down to listen to cosy little sermons about the love of God. What, I asked myself, were they doing for people like the lad whose pathetic dead body I had just been to witness? Have they even any idea, I wonder, about what is actually going on all around them? Would they want to do something if they did? I suppose the question that I really want answered is, what can we as Christian churches do to reach out to these people in our community? Do we really care?"

Peter and David had sat silently through Jim's obviously heartfelt description of his conviction and vision. They were impressed. Here was a Christian man, right at the cutting-edge of the drugs problem that was blighting Fraserburgh, with the expressed desire to see some positive action taken about it.

The Acting Chief Inspector prefaced his final question with a statement of confidence in the two men before him. "You men have some experience of what I am talking about here. You are in touch with the situation. Will you help me organise something amongst the churches? If we could even make them aware of the extent of the problem so that they could start praying intelligently it would be a start."

It was an inspiring, comprehensive, Christian initiative, and David and Peter were only too happy to assist in any way possible to see it advanced.

In less than a month after that initial meeting a letter was sent out inviting all the churches in Fraserburgh and the surrounding villages to send a representative to an exploratory meeting with a two-fold purpose. It was to familiarise them with the need for Christian care and the opportunities for outreach amongst a very vulnerable section of local society, and to ask for suggestions as to how the state of affairs could best be addressed.

The response was encouraging. Thirty-seven people turned up for that inaugural, informative and challenging session in Fraserburgh Police Station. Some had come out of a vague Christian curiosity. They had heard that there was a 'drugs problem' out there somewhere and it would be 'nice' to be able to do something to help. Others, like David and Helen, whose family circumstances had seen them involuntarily sucked into the centre of the situation, attended out of a deep sense of commitment. They were thrilled that somebody had both the verve and the vision to try and bring the need of the community to the attention of the churches.

Whatever their motivation for attending, when Acting Chief Inspector Urquhart and two other Christian policemen outlined, with occasional graphic illustrations, the scale of the problem virtually on their church doorsteps there was a unanimous consensus that some action needed to be taken. And it was.

By the close of this preliminary gathering of church representatives an action committee had been selected and the Inter-Church Drugs Strategy Group established.

Their first aim was to create an awareness of the scope of the problem in the town amongst its church congregations. This in turn was to lead to special prayer sessions being arranged in different districts where concerned Christians could come together to pray earnestly for specific issues.

One of these was that the police would succeed in coming to grips with the criminal element in the overall drugs scenario. Their concern was that they would be able to apprehend those actually supplying the drugs to the young people of Fraserburgh.

As the Inter-Church Drugs Strategy Group began to awaken an awareness of the drug problem in the community they learnt of two young men who had acquired a prime site on one of the town's main thoroughfares with a view to opening a drop-in centre for addicts.

The group offered to help Ben and Victor furnish and equip these premises. This would be an ideal neutral location in which to meet those with drug related difficulties. It would not only be a haven for people anxious to break the bonds of addiction but caring staff could also provide support for their families.

When the vision of this proposed upstairs retreat on Broad Street was announced in the churches in the area, donations, both of money and furniture and fittings began to come in. Local Christian tradesmen from a variety of church backgrounds formed a willing band of workers who toiled away voluntarily after hours to install new plumbing and wiring, do all the necessary carpentry, and finally paint the premises.

After some months of dedicated work, and a number of generous donations, the set of upstairs rooms became transformed into an attractive retreat from the bustling world down on the street outside.

The organisers of this innovative project recognised that the naming of such a venue could be vitally important. Its name would have to reflect its Christian ethos without sounding too religious or church-related. After some prayerful consideration they decided to call their new sanctuary of support, this place that would hopefully prove a port in the storm to many who were being smashed to pieces in the tempests of life, The Solid Rock Café.

A graphic designer produced a series of modern style black and white posters each depicting a real life situation, and each subtly incorporating the words Solid Rock somewhere in its composition.

The Solid Rock Café had been carefully and prayerfully planned. Its tasteful but imaginative layout and attractive Christian ambience would no doubt prove appealing to those in need of a haven of rest.

It was opened to the public on January 1 st 2000.

Fraserburgh had its own very worthwhile Millennium Project courtesy of a number of men of dedication and discernment, and the Inter-Church Drugs Strategy Group.

Acting Chief Inspector Urquhart was particularly pleased.

The shut up churches had opened up in the centre of town.

God would honour this commitment.

Chapter 13

# THROW ME A ROPE!

Many ordinary, honest men lose their lives at sea, some protecting our freedom, others simply providing our food.

Fishing can be dangerous. One mistake on a fishing boat can prove disastrous. The families of Fraserburgh, both the fathers and sons who fish for a living, and the mothers, wives and daughters who remain behind ashore, live with that knowledge. It is part of their way of life, their culture.

There are many near shaves, too. Most fishermen can tell of times when their lives were in danger, but they were somehow spared an untimely end.

Matthew Runcie had more than one 'close call' in his days at sea. He had left school to go fishing because, as he told his mum, he needed the money. Although having reasonable wages for a lad of his age, however, he never had any surplus to save. Every penny he earned was spent on buying drugs to satisfy his addiction. The judge's solemn warning had made no difference to him. He was compelled to satisfy his craving. So whatever the cost in round-the-clock physical effort, or the ever-present perils of the sea, Matthew had to sail out with the fishing fleet.

One summer day he was fifty miles out into the North Sea aboard the 'Bountiful' when he was involved in a series of events which could have had a tragic outcome.

The 'Bountiful' carried a crew of four. There was the skipper, the mate, Matthew the deck hand and a 'chance-shotter.' These were men who were employed as casual labour by the skippers to cover for holidays and absences.

Two nets were being shot and then hauled in again over the back of the boat in a system known as twin-rig trawling. There was no net drum on that particular boat and so the nets had to be thrown over the stern by hand.

The nets were pulled aboard, emptied of their catch and then replaced in the sea every five hours. It was while Matthew was watching his running net as it disappeared over the stern that the unexpected occurred.

He was on one side of the boat, and the chance-shotter on the other, each of them in charge of a net, when Matthew noticed that the gear had become snarled up. The dog-rope had become caught up, on its way out, on the wrong side of the clump, an arrangement of chains on the deck. The clump was the last piece of equipment to fall over the stern as its function was to keep the port and starboard nets apart.

Matthew then did something which he had done dozens of times before without even thinking about it. He jumped over the running net to free the entangled dog-rope and allow the net to continue its slide into the sea astern.

Having released the rope, and satisfied himself that the operation was continuing smoothly, Matthew jumped backwards in an attempt to return to his original position.

It was then that the problem arose.

He failed to jump either high enough or far enough to clear the running net and one of his legs became completely enmeshed in the headline sweep, one of the ropes used to attach the nets to the clump. With the momentum of the boat going forward, and the weight and speed of the net in which he had become ensnared running backward, Matthew could feel himself being pulled towards the stern.

He paused momentarily, while his legs were pulled against

the back of the boat, and it was in that moment that he yelled, "Knock the boat out of gear!"

Nobody heard him. So nothing happened.

The skipper couldn't hear him for the noise in the wheelhouse, the mate was out of earshot, and the chance-shotter was concentrating on his own net and only looked up in time to see the deckhand who had been working away beside him being catapulted into the sea.

Matthew knew what was happening but was powerless to prevent it.

When he came to the surface he found that his overboard plunge had freed him from the restricting ropes so he shook the water from his hair and face and looked around.

It was a chilling, sickening feeling. He was out in the North Sea and the boat from which he had been launched into the water was some distance away, and going farther away. He tried to swim towards it but although he was a strong swimmer he could make no progress. The man overboard was still dressed in his oilskin jacket and boots and as the boots filled with water it became almost impossible either to move his legs or kick off the boots.

A dazed looking chance-shotter came to the back of the 'Bountiful' and stared across at the head bobbing about in the sea.

"Throw me a rope!" Matthew yelled.

Still he stood, stupefied.

"Throw me a rope!" Matthew repeated, even more loudly, wondering why the chance-shotter hadn't shot off straight away.

When he did disappear from view a few seconds later Matthew thought he had got the message and expected him to reappear in a matter of seconds to throw a rope over the side to pull him back aboard, but he didn't. What Matthew

didn't realise was that since it was only the man's first trip out
on that boat he hadn't a clue where the ropes were stored!

He had, though, done the next best thing. He had run to
tell the skipper.

Within minutes, although it seemed much longer to
Matthew who was struggling to stay afloat, greatly encumbered
by his heavy fisherman's garb, the throb of the engines ceased.
The boat was stopping. Soon the skipper appeared at the rail.
He was carrying Matthew's only hope of a rescue. A rope.

Matthew was glad to see him. The skipper was an
experienced seafarer. He knew what to do.

The first throw of the rope dropped short. So did the
second. Matthew struggled to swim forward and at the third
attempt the coiled, snaking rope slapped onto the surface of
the water nearly beside him.

He reached out and grabbed it gladly. The rope was wet
and slippery and so were Matthew's gloves. They kept sliding
as he attempted to hold on and haul himself towards the boat.
It was hard to get a good grip.

The skipper and the chance-shotter were by then both at
the other end, dragging him in. He was being rescued.

On reaching the side of the vessel Matthew had great
difficulty climbing aboard. His clothes were sodden, his boots
were full of water and three times their normal weight, and
the rail was greasy and slimy, a by-product of the fishing.

Appreciating his predicament, and anxious to see
'Bountiful' carry on about her business as soon as possible, the
skipper leaned over, caught his deckhand by the scruff of the
neck and trailed him unceremoniously in over the side-rail.

Matthew half-clambered, half-collapsed, on to the deck
and the skipper enquired, "Are you O.K?"

"Aye, I think so," Matthew replied, gasping for breath.

The skipper immediately turned away. Having assured

himself that his deckhand was well enough to speak, and was therefore probably liable to survive, he was heading back to the wheelhouse. Soon all the machinery began to whirr again. Normal service had been resumed. There was no time to waste.

Matthew slithered across the deck to sit for a moment until he came to. He was shivering violently, involuntarily, from a combination of fear, shock and the icy cold water in which he had just treated himself to a dip.

He pulled off his sea-boots and poured the water out onto the deck beside him. Five minutes later, when the shakes had subsided sufficiently to allow him to stand, he went below, changed his clothes, and returned to his station on deck, helping to sort the last catch.

There was no time for rest or reflection on this job.

Had Matthew cared to cast his mind back to all the messages he had heard in childhood, or had he been aware of all the Christian people who were praying passionately for the Runcie family, he would probably have acknowledged that God had spared his life.

He had been thrown a rope, and the rope had brought hope.

Matthew still had a future.

There remained the possibility of deliverance from the craving for drugs, which had assumed complete control of his life.

The lifeline of salvation was still there to be grasped.

Matthew didn't see it that way, though.

He told the mate later on that day, "I was dead lucky there I can tell you!"

Chapter 14

# A BIT OF STRESS NEVER DID ANYBODY ANY HARM!

By the end of 1999, David the dauntless dad was struggling to cope in every area of his life. He was continuing to try and hide his mounting anxiety in increased activity. Should it be extra cases to be taken on at work, extra meetings to be arranged or addressed at the Church, or extra projects with Christian Faith Ministries, he was always up for it. Anything, anytime, anywhere remained his motto, and the more mental and emotional involvement the engagement or appointment demanded the better.

Signs of weakness had started to show, though.

Chinks had begun to appear in the armour of the valiant Christian volunteer.

He had so much on his mind that he was beginning to forget simple facts, both at home and at work. He had to sit for ages sometimes to remember how to perform simple procedures. And he could never, *ever,* find his car keys, especially when he was in a hurry!

This endless round of energetic escapism led to a strange spiritual detachment. David was speaking at more meetings than ever before, and singing at more church functions than ever before, and yet living a more fruitless, aimless Christian life than ever before. It was as though his head and his heart belonged to two different bodies. David had perfected the practice of going through the motions with all the outward ardour he could muster, but with very little inner commitment or conviction.

His colleagues at work had, for more than a year now, begun to notice that David wasn't performing up to his usual high standard. He was leaving jobs unfinished and cases unresolved. It was peculiar, for the man who had once seemed so confident appeared to have lost the ability to either come to logical conclusions or make important decisions.

Bet, his secretary, who was well aware of the disturbing situation at home, was worried about him. "Are you all right David?" she would enquire when she saw that fatigued, faraway look in his eyes.

"Of course I'm all right, Bet," he would reply, trying his best to sound as though he meant it.

Others of the senior staff remarked, separately and on different occasions, "David, are you sure you are not stressed out? You certainly look it and sound it sometimes."

This comment invariably invoked the same response from David.

"There is no such thing as being stressed out," he would contend, with an over-insistence usually indicative of under-confidence. "This idea of being stressed out is nothing but a figment of the lazy man's imagination. A bit of stress never did anybody any harm!"

To a certain extent he was right. Moderate stress seems to serve as an impetus for action in some cases with some people, but David's stress levels could never have been classed as moderate, by any standards. They were extreme.

In the few private, reflective moments he permitted himself, and especially after he had failed to do what was expected of him, or what he expected of himself, for the third or fourth time in a day, he would acknowledge secretly that he was in difficulty.

"If I don't get a grip on myself I don't know where I am going to end up," he would admit.

That was the danger, but what was the alternative?

To spend more time relaxing at home, the obvious answer, was not an option. David still maintained that his only hope of mental and emotional survival was to remain as remote as possible from the persistent problems in the family.

It couldn't go on forever.

Something had to give, sometime, somewhere.

And it did, one winter night.

It had been a busy weekend. Unlike many who work during the week and unwind at the weekends, David often found himself totally involved in all kinds of Christian activity over the weekend too. It was endless.

On Sunday 27 th February 2000, he attended to his usual Church commitments in the morning. In the evening he was singing with his friends in the male quartet, and then giving the closing address in Calvary Church in Fraserburgh.

On the Monday evening the quartet was booked to sing a few pieces at a special service in Peterhead Baptist Church. David had felt drained during that day at work but that in itself wasn't unusual. He was usually washed out after the weekend. As the day progressed he began to feel sick and actually considered going home to bed. He couldn't give in, though. That would be admitting defeat, and letting the other three members of their little singing group down as well

To save time, and to avoid having to go home, he skipped a meal, changed his clothes in the office and drove to meet the others at the Baptist Church in Peterhead.

When the time came for the quartet to take part David stood up with the others and sang as usual. It was when he returned to his seat that his head began to spin.

The speaker for the evening had begun his address when

David discovered that he couldn't concentrate on what he was saying. The sound of his voice seemed to waft across in echoes as though the preacher had decided to deliver his sermon in a cave.

Waves of nausea swept over him. He felt as though he was going to faint.

There was a growing compulsion to close his eyes and let go. A combined sense of responsibility and respectability opposed that opt-out clause. 'You can't just conk out here! Not in a meeting!' it reminded him.

The time came, however, when David realised that he was going to have to get out. He was either going to pass out or be sick, and he found neither prospect particularly pleasing.

He attempted to rise, and that was the last thing he remembered.

It was then that he collapsed.

When he recovered a hazy consciousness, David was in a back room at the church and his friends from the quartet were discussing arrangements for driving him home. Although he had been unaware of it at the time one of the group who had been sitting beside him had been keeping an eye on him. David's head had almost fallen onto his shoulder at one stage, alerting him to the fact that all was not well with his singing partner.

Helen returned from a committee meeting of the Solid Rock Café to find her husband, whom she had thought to be in Peterhead, in bed.

On hearing of his collapse in the Church at Peterhead and of how one of the men had driven him home and another had brought his car home, Helen was sorry, but in a certain sense not surprised. "It had to come, David," she told him. "Nobody could keep up the pace you were going at for ever. You will have to go to the doctor in the morning."

When he did visit his GP in the morning the doctor told him that he was physically and mentally exhausted, and depressed. She recommended that David attend a course of counselling, prescribed a courses of medication, and ordered complete and absolute rest from all activity, at work, at church and at home.

The medicine would be easy to take, total respite he would find unusual though probably not impossible, but David didn't fancy the idea of counselling. He reckoned that his faith in God and the prayers of his many Christian friends could compensate for any lack of human counselling, so he asked if that could be deferred as an option, at least in the meantime.

The news of David's breakdown spread rapidly amongst those who knew him, from all aspects of his life.

His Christian friends, and many of the churches in which the Runcie family had sung more than ten years before, added father to the sons, already on their prayer list.

All his colleagues at work were extremely supportive. They told him not to consider returning until he was completely recovered. "Take as long as you need off," they said, "and even when you do come back you could ease yourself into the routine a day, or two days, a week at the start. We will understand too if you need time out to do something with the boys. All you have to do is tell us and take it!"

That was reassuring. His managers knew that he would recover in time, and with care.

The first week at home was difficult. Everything appeared totally black.

David was so weak that all he wanted to do was lie around. He had no enthusiasm for anything, and this was inclined to worry him. The fact that he was at home, the very location he had been studiously avoiding where possible for at least two years, didn't help either. The boys were still around, when not at sea, and the suspicion that they were continuing to buy and use heroin, wasn't an ideal pick-me-up.

Perhaps the most perplexing element in the entire situation was that he found he couldn't concentrate on reading the Bible. Nor would his mind allow him to order his thoughts in any kind of intelligent way to permit him to pour out his anguished soul to God in prayer.

He had told the doctor that he didn't need counselling, presuming that he would be able to organise his own tailor-made course of treatment through Bible reading and prayer. Now, it seemed that he was incapable of doing either!

This continuing spiritual aloofness was compensated for, at least in measure, by the visits of kind Christians from many of the various fellowships in and around Fraserburgh. David was soon to discover, though, that he could only cope with these visits in small doses. Short scripture readings and brief to the point prayers he found uplifting, but intricate Bible expositions were totally lost on him.

David was so dejected and bewildered in those early days of his illness that there was one verse, often quoted by well-meaning visitors, with which he found it hard to come to terms. The gist of the idea was, ' You feel wrecked at the minute, David, but don't worry. Just remember, the Scripture says that 'all things work together for good to them that love God"

That was fine to say, when you were feeling O.K. but in his position nothing seemed to be working together for anything, not to mention all things working together for good!

In less than a fortnight, though, the outlook appeared somewhat brighter.

Persistent fervent prayer by Christians from many denominations, Helen's care, medication, and the interest and concern of his workmates all began to have a positive effect.

Gradually, as David's physical strength began to increase, so too, did his interest in spiritual and practical matters all around him.

He found it possible to pray again, with the assurance that his petitions were being heard in heaven, not just bouncing off the ceiling. And he had begun to derive solace from a renewed interest in reading the Scriptures. His spiritual appetite was returning.

As he became mentally more focussed David wanted to be involved again. The old desire to be doing something was back, so he started to set himself targets.

His first project was to tidy his tool cupboard in the garage, which had become rather neglected. In addition to his other many interests David loved to work in wood and he had many tools. With so much else going on his store was in a mess.

Now he had the time to sort it out to his satisfaction. He didn't have either the physical endurance or the powers of concentration to remain at any job for too long so this target was met in a systematic, scheduled way, one shelf per day.

After six weeks at home David considered himself fit to return to his office and resume work on a full programme.

He had been restored to health, and had learnt a lesson.

From now on he would take life a lot easier, and spend more time alone with the Lord, instead of rushing hither and thither in His service.

Those were sensible, honourable aims.

But were they feasible or achievable?

There were still heroin addicts in his house.

# Chapter 15

# WHY? WHY? WHY?

As David continued to regain his ability to work while constantly monitoring his level of involvement in all essential activity, his wife had begun to ask awkward questions.

Helen's Christian friends had often commended her fortitude with her faith under such sustained fire. When she attended a meeting she always tried to be positive when requesting 'prayer for the boys.'

What those people didn't realise was that she was merely trying to put a brave face on the desperate problems that were tearing her heart and soul to bits. She had heard so many sermons about God's presence with His people in all the circumstances of life that she had all the right answers when friends showed sympathy for her situation.

"God is in control of our lives and He has promised never to leave us or forsake us. Our trust is in Him," she affirmed confidently.

"This is a time of testing for us," she told Margaret, a lady from the church in whom she confided on some of the darkest days. "I am sure that we will eventually come out at the other end of all of this like gold tried in the fire, to shine purer and brighter for God."

Despite all her apparent spiritual steadfastness, nothing ever seemed to become any easier, however. It was now six years since the Saturday night they had arrived home to find Jonathan drunk and this whole sorry mess had being going on since then. Things had just been limping from bad to worse. She had never been able to detect even the faintest flicker of light at the end of the tunnel.

Then came David's collapse.

It was horrendous to have to admit that two of her sons were confirmed heroin addicts, but when her husband was healthy and well she could always pour out her woes to him whenever she saw him. This was usually either late at night when he came in, exhausted, or early in the morning before he hurried out, half-rested. At least he was there, to share, and care.

By early March 2000 that scene had all changed. David was at home all the time now and in need of constant tender loving care. Helen was well qualified and only too happy to provide this, but it was an additional burden on overstretched emotions.

It was during those days, with her husband ill, and her sons more handicap than help, that the questions began to well up in Helen's heart, in spite of all her best efforts to suppress them.

Why was all this happening to them when they were working so hard in Christian service?

Why was God not answering the millions of prayers He had heard about their family?

Why was it taking so long?

Why did others seem to be getting it so easy compared to them? People who weren't doing half as much as they were…

Why? Why? Why?

These questions continued to plague her, clouding over the comforting sunlight of spiritual hope that had kept her going even through the most trying experiences up until then.

One evening in May, after a particularly depressing day, Helen felt that she needed to open the floodgates of her repressed emotions and irritating reservations to somebody. She didn't, however, want to confide in a 'Yes man or woman,' somebody who would say all the things she wanted them to say and trot out a string of platitudes about everything turning 'out O.K. in the end.' Like David, a few months before, she had reached the depths of despair, where the only colour she could ever see in her circumstances was black.

Helen's confidant would have to be someone whose personal integrity and spiritual insight she respected. After giving the matter some thought she eventually decided to share her profound concerns with Dr. Sam Gordon, an esteemed Christian writer and broadcaster.

Sam had conducted Bible teaching sessions in Bethesda Evangelical Church on many occasions, had stayed over with the family more than once and had learnt to pay particular attention to the whereabouts of his wallet. He was well aware of the distressing state of affairs in David and Helen's home. They had shared their heartbreak with him, often tearfully, on his overnight stops.

It had been difficult that day, and with more questions than answers in her mind Helen sat down at the word-processor and let her feelings flow out freely onto the patiently waiting paper.

*'Tell me, Sam,'* she wrote, *'is it really a sin for a child of God, who genuinely believes that God is in control, to be so overwhelmed as I feel today with the situation that our boys are in, that I want to ask* **WHY?** *I feel so burdened for them today that my heart is physically aching, and the tears are readily flowing, even as I write this.*

*Honestly, it's not often that I feel I need to question God, (I feel guilty that I am today) and the way is not always so hard, but today just seems to be one of those days when the burden seems heavier than usual*

*Even today as I search my own heart, God knows that we have sought to bring them up to love Him and His Word. Even as I write this down I feel bad for questioning Him. Why, when we feel that we have been faithful in teaching them the truths from His Word has He not drawn them to Himself? The waiting for them to return to their own border is so hard. (Jeremiah 31:16&17)*

*As I weep for them, the cry of my own heart is that I may know Him...'*

Helen posted the letter but it was a few weeks before she received a reply. What she was not to know was that at the time she had felt the urge to pour out her innermost spiritual struggles in print, Dr. Gordon was abroad on a preaching tour.

He attended to the matter with great haste, however, on his return, recognising in Helen's letter the honest expression of an anguished soul. His reply was encouraging.

*'The fact that you love your boys and that you have both given your very best for them is indicative of the heart you both have for them in the Lord, Helen,'* came the response. *'While at this point in time they appear to have little or no interest in the things of God causes you immense concern. That is perfectly understandable... The fact is, and it's easy for me to say it, they are in the Lord's hands and I firmly believe that the Lord will, in His own good time, answer your prayers. You have done all that you possibly can. Your only option is to continue to uphold them in prayer and leave the results down to the timing of the Lord. At the end of the day, He will honour your love and faithfulness to Himself and to the family and He will do it in a way that may even surprise you.*

*Sure, God is sovereign; that is true – but you are only human! Even on the cross, the Lord Jesus posed the big question, 'Why?' Because He is who He is, that makes it all the more remarkable... The fact that you do it, and the fact that I do it, shows our utter dependence upon Him, and rather than being a cause for guilt, it should indicate our humble awareness that we can't go on without His aid. If that's how He felt at a critical juncture in His life, it should come as no surprise to us that we feel overwhelmed with the challenges in our lives from time to time...'*

This was reassuring. It was good to realise that her feelings were indeed 'normal.' And the thought that Her Saviour had even asked 'Why?' when on the cross, was something she had never contemplated before, and a concept that helped set her mind at ease.

After receiving that letter, and having come to consider their position both rationally and prayerfully, David and Helen sat down together one evening and agreed a painful policy decision. They recognised the need to be seen to be in control of all that was taking place under their roof and also to present a united front to the boys in relation to their drug-taking habits. This was to prevent a wedge being driven between them when one or other of the boys could claim, 'That's not what dad said,' or, 'Mum would never go along with that.'

They pledged to dispose, without question, of any illegal substance they found in the house, and agreed, not without much heart-searching, that if they ever found any of the boys actually *using* heroin in the house, he would be asked to leave until he sorted himself out.

This nearly broke Helen's heart. She knew in her head that it was the only option left to them. That was the theory, substantiated by common sense.

How would it work out, though, if they were actually called upon to put it into practice?

Chapter 16
# THAT'S MINE AND I WANT IT!

In early July 2000 Jonathan announced that he was going with three friends to 'T In The Park,' a rock music festival, down south in Kinross.

"And who are the friends?" his mum was anxious to know.

Jonathan listed the name of the local lads who were to be his companions for the trip. They would never have been her first choice of friends for her son, and she certainly wouldn't have chosen a pop festival as a special treat for him either. Helen could at least cling, for the slightest crumb of comfort, to the belief that the chap who was to be driving the car wasn't on drugs. She couldn't be sure about the other two, but she was, regrettably, sure about Jonathan.

"And where will you be sleeping?" mother enquired after learning that 'T In The Park' was to be a weekend event.

"We're taking a tent with us. We will be sleeping in it for the two nights," her son went on to inform her.

"Oh no, Jonathan!" was Helen's instant reaction.

"Oh yes, mum!" was Jonathan's equally immediate and emphatic retort as he walked out.

Next weekend he was away.

Jonathan was due to go back to sea soon after his return from Kinross. He was lying on his bed one morning and his mum was in chatting to him, but making a thorough inspection of the drawers in the simple chest in his room as she did so.

This had become normal practice for her.

All three boys had been warned of the new rules. Any drugs found in the house would be confiscated and anyone found actually using heroin would be asked to leave until he saw sense.

In her earlier checks in every drawer she considered suspect, and every other nook and cranny which could have been considered a hiding place, Helen had discovered a few home made hash pipes, cigarette butts and lighters. She had never found any drugs, though.

That was not until that particular day.

As she rummaged through an untidy collection of underwear, CD's and dog-eared, drink-stained magazines she noticed a peculiar block of a strange substance, painstakingly positioned right in the back corner of a drawer.

Helen reached in and lifted it out for closer examination. It was like an overgrown Oxo cube. Although never having come across a piece that size before she recognised it for what it was. It was hash, cannabis resin, in a chunk so big that she could barely close her hand on it.

Turning to face Jonathan, where he was lying on top of the bed, she asked pointedly, "Where on earth did you get this lump of stuff?"

When he realised that she had found his block of hash, Jonathan panicked. He jumped up and tried to grab it from his mum who had backed against the wall with her son's latest purchase behind her back.

"Give me that! Give me that!" he began to shout, making one monster bound across to block the door so that his mum couldn't make a speedy exit. "That's mine and I want it! It's not yours. You have no business taking my stuff! I insist that you hand it over to me right now! Straightaway! Immediately!"

"No, Jonathan. You are not having it," Helen maintained her stance, trying to remain unruffled. "Your dad and I have warned all of you that if we ever found any of this rubbish in the house you wouldn't be getting it back. And I have found it so I am keeping it until we dispose of it."

Jonathan then became really angry. There was another element in the equation that his mum hadn't cared to consider, but which he was prepared to point out to her, as powerfully as possible. "Do you realise how much that thing in your hand cost me?" he yelled, his voice ending in a piercing shriek. "Have you any idea how much I paid for that?"

"No, Jonathan. I have no idea how much you paid for it, and to tell you the truth, I don't care, but if you were stupid enough to spend your money on it, that is your affair. The fact of the matter is I have found it in this house, and I will not be giving it back to you!" his mum told him. Then taking a step forward she ordered, "Now let me out!"

It was a chance to take, but Jonathan moved away from the door, almost automatically in response to her sharp command, and Helen hurried down the stairs.

"Oh God, help!" she prayed inwardly, urgently.

It had suddenly dawned on her that she was alone in the house with Jonathan, who was the tallest of her three boys, and infinitely stronger than she was. If he became any more frantic, that mounting frenzy might just cause him to step across the fine line between respect and reprisal. Then she would be in big trouble. He could easily wrest the block of hash from her and possibly injure her badly in the process.

"Oh God, help!" she breathed inwardly again, even more urgently.

Helen transferred the lump in her hand to her pocket and by the time Jonathan arrived down in the kitchen her hands were free.

"Where is it? I want it!" he continued to demand, but his mum was encouraged to note that he seemed to have calmed just a little. He now appeared more disappointed than angry, more crying than crazy.

It was hard to remain cool in such a situation, but Helen struggled to sound ever so matter of fact as she pronounced, not for the first time. "No, Jonathan. You are not having it back. I said it and I mean it. You may as well just forget it."

When Jonathan finally realised that his expensive purchase would have to be written off he turned and stormed out into the hall, banging the door furiously after him.

Helen rushed off to hide the hash and when she had done so sat down for a cup of coffee and a moment's reflection.

It had been an unpleasant confrontation but she had upheld the principle that David and she had agreed. The cannabis had been confiscated.

"Thank you, Lord," she said, softly.

When David arrived in from work after five o'clock Helen recounted the incident and he asked, "Where is it now?"

"I will soon dispose of this," he went on resolutely after Helen had told him where she had hidden Jonathan's expensive purchase and he had retrieved it.

His mother was ill at that time and David and Helen had planned to go and visit her in Aberdeen Royal Infirmary later that evening. They took the block of hash with them and David slowed down at one point as he was driving along in a remote rural area, opened the window and tossed it into a field of cows.

"I wonder what will happen if a cow eats that stuff?" he remarked to Helen. They had a laugh together as they drove on again.

"What will the milk taste like?" his wife replied, carrying the idea through to its ultimate comical conclusion.

David's modified lifestyle, his evening visit to his mother, and his relative detachment from the events of the day meant that he had no trouble sleeping that night on his return from Aberdeen.

His wife found sleep much more elusive, though. She lay

tossing and turning, reliving the encounter with Jonathan, remembering every word, every action, every intonation.

She wondered what she would have done if she had come across Jonathan actually smoking the hash.

She reflected on just how vulnerable she had been, a small woman facing up to a big, angry lad. It was then, as she continued to dwell on how she had been protected during the incident that her mind turned to a song she hadn't heard for many years.

Helen had often sat as a child with her ear glued to the old record player, listening to the words of a prized collection of 78rpm records. And it was the final words of one of those old sacred songs that kept repeating themselves over and over in her mind as she lay there in mental turmoil.

'Tenderly He watches over you

Every step, every mile of the way,' was how it began, and how it ended, she recalled.

These words and the tune came back to her easily, and as Helen began to sing them to herself in bed she found them so comforting. She remembered some of the remaining words, but not them all. Helen just couldn't get the complete lyrics into her head. Snippets of it, though, returned.

There was another line that said, 'When you're weak, when you're strong.'

That was how she had felt that afternoon. Incredibly weak and inadequate, but God had been her strength.

Consoled by the reminder that God was watching over her, in spite of the trauma that had become her everyday life, Helen drifted off to sleep.

Next day as she worked around the house she kept humming the tune to herself, but still she hadn't all the words. She thought she knew where she could find them, though.

An excursion up to, and a forage through, the loft, brought the required result. There she discovered an old 'single,' stashed away with dozens of others, discarded to make way for the day of the compact disc.

Helen brought it downstairs and began to play it, over and over again. Now she could hear all the words, and having had her memory refreshed she soon had it all off by heart once more.

Soon she was singing softly, wherever she went, or whatever she was doing,

> Tenderly He watches over you,
> Every step, every mile of the way,
> Like a mother watching o'er her baby,
> He is near you every hour of the day.
>
> When you're weak, when you're strong,
> When you're right when you're wrong,
> In your joy, in your pain,
> When you lose and when you gain.
>
> Long before time began,
> You were part of His plan,
> Let no fear cloud your brow,
> He will not forsake you now.
> Tenderly He watches over you,
> Every step, every mile of the way.

Helen derived tremendous comfort from those words for days.

They reminded her of two tremendous truths.

God was still in control, and He still cared for her, whatever happened.

Or whatever lay ahead.

Chapter 17
# IT'S MAKE YOUR MIND UP TIME!

It was good that God was 'tenderly watching over' His anxious child for Helen had a lot on her mind by mid-July 2000.

She had gone eyeball-to-eyeball with Jonathan, just before he set out on a fishing trip to sea, on one of the issues upon which her husband and she had agreed to make a stand. That was the question of the confiscation of all drugs found in the house. Worse still, she was awaiting a decision on the other potentially more heartbreaking one when Matthew returned from his next trip.

Just over a week before the post-'T In The Park' altercation with her youngest son, Helen had discovered Matthew in his bedroom surrounded by all the trappings of a heroin 'fix.' There were scraps of tinfoil scattered around the floor with intricate patterns of zigzag lines burnt all over them.

There could be no doubt about it.

Matthew had been 'chasing the dragon.'

Helen had been so upset that she had burst out in tears.

An incompatible emotional mix of downright stupidity at being caught and loyalty to his careworn mum left Matthew feeling sick at himself.

He knew the score.

The rule, about which all three boys had received adequate warnings, had been broken. Mum had just come across him 'using' again, 'under our roof', one of his dad's favourite phrases to describe the applicable borders of this most recent dictum. So the conditions it carried with it would have to be applied. The price would have to be paid.

This was decision day for Helen. There could be no compromise.

It was day one of a critical period for Matthew, too, as she had told him.

"You are going away to sea this evening," she had said, "and before you come back in ten days time I will expect you to have decided whether you want to live here or not in the future. The choice is simple. Either you do something about your drug taking or you look out for alternative accommodation. Your dad has three application forms for council houses, one for each of you, should you have to be asked to leave. All you have to do is sign it and he will do the rest."

"Ach mum," Matthew had begun to protest. "That's not fair to give me an ultimatum like that!"

"Fair or not, ten days will give you plenty of time," Helen had countered, prepared to give no quarter. It was heart wrenching for her, but she knew the issue had to be faced, and their stipulations carried out to the letter. "I'm sorry Matthew, but it's make your mind up time!"

With that Helen turned and left the room to sit and have a quiet cry to herself in the corner of the lounge. Matthew had been left semi-stunned in his bedroom, the full import of her final emphatic statement echoing in his ears.

That had been ten days ago. The joust with Jonathan had happened when Matthew was away. Now he would be home anytime…

When he came, though, he caught his mum by surprise.

It was a beautiful, sunny, July day, with not a cloud in the sky. Helen was out in the back garden hanging out the washing when he came out through the back door and straight across to stand beside her.

"Hi, Matthew. How did your trip go? Are you O.K?" she

enquired, automatically. In the thrill of seeing her son home safely from the sea once more she had forgotten that she was expecting him to inform her of an important decision he was supposed to have made.

Matthew hadn't forgotten, however.

It would appear that he had chosen to ignore his mum's welcoming pleasantries for his first words were, "By the way, I have been thinking about what you said."

"What are you on about, Matthew?" Helen asked him, still unaware that he was trying to introduce the response she had demanded, and was dreading.

Helen had by then paused in her pegging and Matthew looked her straight in the eye before replying, "You said that I had to either sort my problem out or get out. Is that not right?"

"Aye, that's right," his mum agreed, her heart sinking to the soles of her sandals. You've done it now, she thought. He's just about to tell you he's moving out!

It was a few seconds before she dared ask, again trying to sound as unperturbed as possible, but butterflies had begun to flutter in her stomach, "Well, what is your decision?"

"I want to apply to Teen Challenge," he said softly, still fixing her with his eye.

"Oh Matthew, I'm so pleased," Helen replied, trying to control her mounting emotions. She wasn't quite sure whether she wanted to laugh or cry. All she knew was that she was possessed with an overwhelming urge, which she managed to resist in the cause of continuing to maintain her businesslike approach, to hug him, and hug him, and hug him.

Teen Challenge is an organisation established by David Wilkerson, author of 'The Cross And The Switchblade.' He started his work amongst drug addicts in New York, and through his ministry many were brought to faith in Christ. Since then Teen Challenge has become an international movement. It is based on the principles that the Gospel is the power of God unto salvation, and that Jesus Christ can still save all those who call upon Him, and deliver them from the chains of addiction that may have bound them for years.

It would be wonderful for Matthew.

"The leaders down at The Solid Rock Café keep a supply of application forms, you will get one from them," his mum went on to tell him, absolutely thrilled.

And just as her disappointment at his drug-taking had made him in a sense unhappy, so her obvious delight at his decision made him feel good, even if only for an hour or two.

Later that afternoon Matthew was sitting out in the sun. He had obviously decided to make the best of the good weather before joining his boat for another fishing trip in a few days time.

Helen called out through the wide open back door to the figure in the sunglasses lying lolling, smoking on the sun-chair, "Do you want a drink or anything, Matthew?"

"No thanks, mum. Not at the minute," her son replied, wearily.

Realising that he was apt to nod off, as he sounded so tired and looked so comfortable, Helen warned him, "If you don't watch out you are going to fall asleep and that cigarette will burn a hole in your T-shirt!"

It had happened before and it looked likely to happen again. And it did.

Helen had turned back and was barely half an hour into the house when she heard a yell of annoyance from the sunbather in the garden.

"Oh no! Here we go again!" she could hear him exclaim. His mum rushed out to see him rubbing frantically at the front of the T-shirt he had just bought himself on his previous trip off, and of which he seemed particularly proud.

His mum's warning had gone unheeded but her prediction had come true.

Matthew had dozed off and the lighted cigarette he had been holding had fallen on to his chest, burning two black holes in his shirt.

When he saw Helen coming across the garden to join him he started to shout out of sheer frustration, "That's it! I've had enough! I've no money, I've no decent clothes, and when I'm at work on the boat I feel like an old-age pensioner! These drugs are messing up my whole life! I am definitely going to Teen Challenge!"

Knowing that it would be unwise to press for too much too soon Helen had obtained a couple of copies of the Teen Challenge application form from the Solid Rock Café, and given them to her son.

Up until that point though, although Matthew had them in his possession, he hadn't actually completed one of them.

"You'd better fill in your form and send it off then," his mum advised gently. "The sooner it's in the sooner you will get away."

When Matthew had gone upstairs to change his shirt Helen sat down at the kitchen table and bowed her head in thanksgiving. "Thank you, Lord, for this amazing answer to prayer," she began happily but humbly. "We can see now that You are beginning to move in Matthew's life. David and I just pray that he will go to Teen Challenge, and above all, whether there or somewhere else, we long that You will draw him to Yourself. Amen."

Matthew was out that evening so Helen seized the opportunity to fill David in on all the details of her afternoon conversation with him and to contact all her Christian prayer partners. She wanted to bring them up to date on this significant change in Matthew's attitude, which only God could have brought about, and beseech them to continue to pray that he would carry out his resolve and actually apply to, and be accepted by, Teen Challenge.

These prayers became all the more fervent and pointed when Helen discovered the application forms, still uncompleted, when Matthew was away off on his next trip to sea. Doubts began to creep in. Was it all a big con? Was he just saying the right things so that he could still stay at home? Or was she trying to rush ahead of the Lord and His perfect will and timing?

Her fears were partially allayed and her questions just half answered a fortnight later. Matthew was at home and two young men from Canada who had been drug-addicts but had become Christians and had seen their lives miraculously turned around, called to see him. They were members of a team on a two-week summer outreach mission with the Solid Rock Café and someone had told them about Matthew.

Helen was glad that Matthew had received them so amicably, and was even more pleased when she heard the sound of laughter and animated conversation coming from the room where the three of them were chatting. Those lads had been were Matthew was, understood how he felt, and could identify with him completely. And when they told him of the transformation God had brought about in their lives through faith in Christ it made a big impression.

His mum's joy increased even further when her son remarked after they had gone, more than an hour later, "I wouldn't mind having what those guys have got!"

Their visit had such an impact on him that he made another move towards reaching out to grasp 'what they had got.'

Matthew filled in the application form for Teen Challenge.

There was only one more step to take, though, and that was going to take either extreme courage on his part or another crisis in his life, plus still more persistent prayer by David and Helen's army of Christian friends, to see enacted.

He had to post it.

Chapter 18
# GEE THANKS, GOD!

It was fine to resolve that he was 'going to apply for Teen Challenge.'

Putting that into practice proved much more difficult than Matthew had ever imagined it would be, though. The declaration had tripped off his tongue so readily more than once, the outward expression of an inward intention. He had no idea of the ferocity of the physical and mental struggle that he would have to endure before seeing it through.

Common sense was telling him that he needed to call a halt, go to rehab, and hopefully build a life for himself, not dominated by drugs. His inner cravings, on the other hand, were for more drugs. It was so hard to break the habit of years. His body was crying out for another 'fix.'

Matthew had become embroiled in a disturbing emotional tug-of-war.

In late August 2000 some of his mates had invited him to go with them to Peterhead to buy some 'stuff.' Looking upon this as an ideal opportunity to lay in a stock of 'gear' before his next trip to sea, Matthew went along.

It was to prove an ill-fated trip.

The local police must have somehow received a tip-off about the car carrying five young people, and their afternoon's 'shopping,' back to Fraserburgh. When the driver and his four happy-go-lucky passengers came to the outskirts of the town they found something there to wipe the laughs from their lips. Two CID cars were stopping the traffic on a major roundabout.

One lad gasped, "It's the police," and all the doors of the car were immediately locked. Some of the occupants of the car swallowed the drugs they had bought straight away, but Matthew didn't.

He had bought two lots of drugs that afternoon. The most of his money had gone on an eighth of an ounce of heroin but he had also treated himself to a 'rock' of crack cocaine. Heroin-addicts are compelled to supply their habit first of all whatever the cost, but if they have a pound or two left over they are often tempted to buy crack or some other more potent drug as an added extra, a special luxury.

As he saw six police officers bearing down upon the car Matthew had two packets of drugs to dispense with. It was important to get rid of the heroin first so he burst his bag and tried furiously to rub his precious purchase into the mat on the floor of the car, hoping that it would disappear into the pile. The 'rock' of crack was smaller so he popped it into his mouth and lodged it below his tongue.

Soon the policemen outside were hammering on the windows of the car, demanding that the doors be opened. The five inside resisted for a while but then, realising that if they didn't do as the police commanded they would burst in anyway, they bowed to the pressure and opened up.

One by one all five people in the vehicle, four boys and a girl, stepped out and were immediately handcuffed by police officers. A superficial examination of the car caused one of the policemen to remark, upon discovering the heroin on the mat at Matthew's feet, "You certainly had a lot of stuff on you, did you not?" He paid little or no attention to Matthew's explanation that it only looked a lot because he had tried to spread it out. There was no way that such a lame excuse would ever wash with experienced drugs squad officers like these.

When the five handcuffed young people arrived down at the local police station they were all separated into individual rooms, searched and then interviewed by specialist officers. Matthew was given a robust cross-examination and despite his protests failed to convince the interrogating team that the drugs he had made a futile attempt to conceal in the carpet of the car were intended solely for his own consumption.

When the questioning was over Matthew was informed that he was being charged with three infringements of the law. The first two and more serious of these were offences for which, with his previous record, he could have been handed down a prison sentence. They were being in possession of a class A drug and intent to supply a class A drug. The other less serious offence was one with which all five occupants of the car were to be charged. It was that of resisting arrest, for failing to open the car doors immediately upon demand.

Matthew was sickened by these charges, but what he didn't know at the time was that his parents were at that moment also being stunned by what was happening at home.

David had just arrived home from work after five o'clock when there was a knock at the door. On opening it he was confronted by three plain-clothes police officers, two men and a woman. "Is this where Matthew Runcie lives?" one of them asked.

"Yes it is," David replied.

"Well I take it you are his father," the spokesman for the three went on.

"Yes, I am, why, what has he done?" the surprised dad was anxious to know.

"He has been apprehended this afternoon with drugs in his possession," the patient policeman went on to explain, producing a folded piece of paper. "We have here a warrant to search this house. May we come in?"

When he gave them permission to enter the three said that they were mainly interested in examining Matthew's room if his dad could direct them to it, and that he was at liberty to watch as they carried out their search.

David showed them to the room, which they went over very carefully but in which they failed to find any incriminating drugs. All they could discover that would in any way link Matthew with the drugs scene were a few scraps of used tinfoil.

When Helen came home from the local supermarket where she had been shopping she was puzzled to find a strange car outside the house, and even more confused to hear strange voices talking to David in one of the downstairs bedrooms when she stepped into the hall. She went into the kitchen to put away her groceries and when her husband joined her after the 'visitors' had gone she enquired, "And what was all that about, David?"

"It's Matthew, he has been caught with heroin on him again," David told her. "That was the drugs squad in to search his room. They didn't find much, though. Only a bit or two of tinfoil."

"Oh no! Not again!" Helen exclaimed in an agony of exasperation.

"Isn't he so stupid, and isn't that so ironic?" she went on before her husband could respond to her initial outburst. "Look at that!"

When David looked 'at that' he discovered that what she was pointing to was Matthew's completed, but still not posted, application form for Teen Challenge.

"If he doesn't soon get away to rehab he is going to end up in prison," she continued flatly. "Where is he now by the way?"

Helen was absolutely worn out with worry.

"He is being held down at the station for questioning, until those three officers report back at least I would think," David told her.

Matthew was indeed still down at the police station and he had been placed in a holding cell.

He was totally broken, and unbelievably bitter.

The cellophane on his crack had started to open up in his mouth and his immediate priority was to transfer it from mouth to pocket now that he was alone, and sure there would be no more searches.

That done he began to consider the situation in which he found himself.

And he started to cry.

He had hit rock bottom with a splat. Then he began, for the first time since he had been saying boyish prayers at his bedside, to address God. This time, though, it was no repetition of a childish adulation. It wasn't 'Jesus, tender shepherd hear me, bless Thy little lamb tonight.'

His vanquished spirit poured out its shattered reactions in one vitriolic, vindictive outburst. According to Matthew, detained in a holding cell charged with serious drugs offences, it was God who was to blame for this sorry state of affairs, not him!

"My life is all in one big mess!" he fumed, tearfully, "and it's all Your fault, God. You are supposed to be a God of love but take a look at me. If You were a loving God You wouldn't let me end up here. You are supposed to be looking after me, and I am even thinking about going to this Teen Challenge thing, too!"

Matthew paused for a moment before looking up to the ceiling of his cell, as though looking up to heaven, and hissing, "Gee thanks, God!"

When that explosion of emotion blew over he sank back

on the hard seat in the cell, exhausted, waiting to be released, and taken home. At least he had given God a bit of his mind, but it hadn't made him feel any better, just worse.

He felt guilty now, at having addressed the God, whose praise he had once joined in singing, all over the country, in such an aggressive, arrogant manner.

There wasn't a lot to talk about when Matthew arrived home at three o'clock in the morning. He knew that his parents would be disgusted with his behaviour yet again, and he was right. David and Helen didn't really know what to do or say, next.

They had spent part of the evening listening to a recording of a hymn that David said had been on 'his mind all day for some reason.'

It was called, 'It's Always Darkest Before the Dawn,' and brought a message of Christian hope for brighter days. As she sat pondering those words after Matthew had retired sheepishly to his bedroom, Helen wondered how much darker things were going to become before the dawn.

When Matthew rose late the next morning his first mission of the day was to leave the house with a letter in his hand. "This is my application to Teen Challenge," he told his mum. "I am taking it down to post it."

Helen's heart missed a beat.

Was this the first faint ray of dawn to streak across the black night sky?

# Chapter 19

# I JUST CAN'T BELIEVE THIS!

In less than a week Matthew had an initial response to his application for a place in Teen Challenge. He was invited to attend for interview at the organisation's centre in Keighley, Yorkshire, on Tuesday 12 th September. Matthew wasn't sure whether he was altogether excited to receive that call to interview or not, when he first saw it in print. What had he let himself in for?

His parents were extremely happy, however, to the extent that David even arranged to have a day off his work to drive him the four hundred miles down to Keighley. Doug, a friend of David and Helen's, offered to go along for company and to share the driving if necessary.

On the day of the interview the party of three set out early in the morning and when they had gone more than a hundred miles stopped at a roadside café between Dundee and Perth for something to eat. Matthew ate little of what had been placed before him, choosing rather to merely pick through it and push it around his plate. He soon excused himself and disappeared through a door marked 'Gents.' When he emerged about ten minutes later the whites of his eyes were showing. He had been in for a 'fix.'

David was annoyed at his son after they had arrived at their destination and Wayne, the manager of the centre, had begun to ask Matthew a number of introductory questions. His head kept falling forward as though he were about to fall asleep. His dad, who had brought him such a long distance to see this man kept elbowing him and kicking him back into something resembling consciousness.

When he became aware of the father's frustrated embarrassment Wayne said to him, "Don't worry about him, David. It is obvious that he has had 'stuff.' I can see that he is 'dipping.' If you and Doug would like to take a walk around the area for half-an-hour or so I will get all the information I need from him."

It was the voice of experience. Wayne had worked with young men like Matthew before.

Recognising that their presence was probably hindering rather than helping the situation, David and Doug set out to explore their surroundings. They hadn't gone far before they were remarking to each other on two outstanding first impressions of the centre. One was how well it was equipped and the other how immaculately it was kept.

"I wouldn't mind coming here for a holiday myself," Doug quipped.

When the interview was over Wayne offered Matthew a place on the Teen Challenge programme. "Keep in touch with us, Matthew," he advised. "I know that will be difficult with your spells at sea, but phone in when you can. It will probably be between four and six weeks before we have a place for you. We will let you know when the time comes."

The leader then offered to take this latest applicant on a tour of the centre and David and Doug were invited to join them. They now had access to some parts they had been unable to visit on their former walkabout and were even more mightily impressed. They complimented Wayne on the high standard of accommodation being offered and the excellent range of facilities available.

"Yes, we are ideally equipped. We have up-to-date

resources and probably more importantly, an experienced staff, so we consider ourselves able to cope with the needs of all the addicts who come to us. Our work is based strictly on Christian principles and anyone coming here must abide by our rules," he told them.

Doug realised, after what the manager had told them, that perhaps this wasn't where he would want to spend his summer holidays next year after all. By the time they were ready to return to the car to commence the long journey north, it had become evident that this Teen Challenge site was run very much as a drugs detox centre. It was not a holiday camp.

He had this fact even further emphasized to him on the way home as he sat idly leafing through the set of rules Matthew had been given. They made it abundantly clear that when anyone agreed to cross the threshold of that establishment his or her only right was to leave. Strict rules of behaviour were laid down, and would be enforced. If these were not obeyed the ultimate option was that the offender would be placed on the next bus or train home.

Matthew wasn't particularly interested in the rules of the regime at Keighley on the trip back to Fraserburgh. His more immediate concern was to put the back seats of his dad's estate car down so that he could stretch out with his head as close to the tailgate as possible. In that position he thought he could 'chase the dragon' for a few miles without anyone noticing. In his desperation he totally forgot that his dad had a rear-view mirror!

How was he going to cope when the call from Keighley came?

When Matthew heard in late September that there would be a place for him on the Teen Challenge programme in mid-October his parents were delighted.

They felt that they had turned the corner at last. The dawn had broken.

God was still on His throne. Prayers were still being heard, and answered. It was so encouraging.

This warm glow of satisfaction had only been allowed to settle in softly around them for six days until it was shattered again...

It was Sunday 1 st October and Helen was out teaching in the Sunday School in Bethesda Evangelical Church. David the dad had stepped into the bedroom of David the son to ask a simple question, only to be stopped dead in the doorway at what he discovered.

His oldest son, the one he had thought wasn't liable to cause his mum and he as much concern as the other pair, was lying asleep on the top of his bed. Three or four pieces of tinfoil with the telltale patterns burnt into them and a rolled up tube of tinfoil with which to inhale the fumes of the heated heroin, a 'tooter,' lay abandoned across his chest. He had slumped into a drug-induced slumber.

David had obviously been 'chasing the dragon.'

On recovering from the initial shock, his dad acted quickly, instinctively and angrily. He found it difficult to repress a recoil of rage.

Taking two giant steps forward he caught young David by the shoulder and shook him violently. His son was forced awake by the intensity of the onslaught. On struggling to open his eyes he found his dad towering over him. His face had a formidable look about it, a strange fusion of fury and incredulity.

"Not you, David! Surely not you!" he was shouting. "I just can't believe this! You who has everything going for you! A good job now in Aberdeen, a fiancée, and the prospect of a decent settled life! Don't tell me you are going to throw it all away for this rubbish!"

Young David lay and listened, as his father, who

considered himself justifiably incensed, told him of his absolute disappointment in, and amazement at, his son's 'unbelievable stupidity.' He had no option, for he was sure that if he attempted to rise his dad would soon set him down again, considering his mood of the moment.

When he had finished his lecture, having used all the words he knew to express disgust and displeasure, and some of them more than once, David the dad withdrew. David the son was left to reflect upon the problems his dad seemed to think he had, and to clear up his room.

Helen arrived home from Sunday School shortly before four o'clock and by then her husband was sitting seething over a cup of coffee.

"Do you know what I have just come upon this afternoon, Helen?" David burst out almost as soon as she came into the house. "I found David using heroin in his bedroom. He had fallen asleep over it and there was tinfoil everywhere. Has he no sense, I wonder?"

"Yes, I knew that he was using," Helen replied, quietly, realising that David had been, understandably, extremely irritated by his discovery.

She went on immediately, worried in case he would vent his obvious anger on her as well. "I had my suspicions aroused and confronted him with it a few weeks ago, but hadn't the courage to tell you. I knew that it was going to come out sometime, somehow, but I was afraid of our policy. How could I bear to see him being put out? It would be awful with all the plans he has for his life. It would just wreck everything."

David mellowed when he saw the anguished predicament of a mother's heart, and asked, "Well what do you think we should do?"

"Can we not talk to him and try and make him see reason?" his wife wanted to know. "It will be better to keep this a secret amongst ourselves in the meantime. I'm sure we can see him weaned off the drugs, possibly with the help of medication."

This was a terrible blow for David and Helen. They knew that they had problems with Matthew and Jonathan, but they had never anticipated having any trouble with David. As far as they were concerned he appeared to be living a reasonably normal life, and making at least some progress in Christian things. They hadn't even considered obtaining Teen Challenge application forms for David. He was hardly ever likely to need them, or so they thought!

What they didn't know, and what came as a sickening shock to find out, was that David had been living a double life, very successfully, right under their noses, for months. On the rare occasions when he had gone to church he had called with a dealer to buy 'gear' on the way. Having attended the service, and done and said all the expected things, he then came home for a 'fix' late at night when everybody else was in bed.

Now they had three confirmed heroin addicts on their hands, but they were soon to have only two of them in the house. Matthew had been told that there was a place for him in Keighley and was invited to commence the Teen Challenge drugs rehabilitation programme on Tuesday 10 th October.

David and Helen, mum and dad, drove him down to Yorkshire once again, but this time it was to leave him there. Having seen him settled in his accommodation, and under the supervision of the centre staff, they prayed that this would prove to be the breakthrough they were so desperately seeking in the family.

Matthew found it hard going at first.

It was difficult coming off the drugs. The Teen Challenge staff, who were trained to deal with such people, administered the prescribed medication, which had been geared towards his specific needs, but it was tough.

His body reacted violently. His mind objected strongly.

He couldn't sleep. Day and night all appeared to merge into one unremitting agony of mind and body.

There were many times when he felt tempted to exercise his only 'right,' and pack it all in and go home. They aren't really teaching me anything new here, he told himself, so what is the point in staying and putting myself through all this misery?

The underlying emphasis of the teaching given was unashamedly Christian, yet Matthew resisted the message robustly at the start.

There were two factors fuelling a genuine fear within him.

Firstly, he didn't want to say he was a Christian without having made any definite commitment, just because it would please his teachers, and possibly even make life a little easier for himself. That would be a cowardly, cheating thing to do, he reckoned. And then there was the question of what would happen in his life if he should accept Jesus into his heart. Would he be strong enough to withstand the temptations all around him, especially the cravings that were driving him crazy? His mum and dad were dedicated, respected Christians. How could he ever be expected to live like them?

The matter came to a head in the early hours of the morning of Wednesday 18 th. Matthew couldn't sleep. He had been in such torment of body, soul, and mind that he had sat up all night watching a video with a staff member. An intense spiritual struggle was now taking place within him, joining the physical and mental torment occasioned by coming off the drugs to help increase the wretchedness. He was wrestling with the question of giving his life to Christ.

One side of him, inspired by a spiritual awareness, was contending that he was incapable of completing the Teen Challenge course alone. You don't have it in you, it insisted.

You need the power of God in your life to help see you through.

That sounded fine and logical until the other voice, that of his natural common sense kept coming up with the alternative argument. If you turn round and tell everybody that you are a Christian, it said, you are going to make one very big fool of yourself. You could never keep it. If you ever dare to say that you are saved you will end up as the laughing stock of all who ever knew you!

Finally, at half-past five in the morning, Matthew yielded to what he knew from his singing and Sunday School days to be the knocking of the Saviour at the door of his heart.

"Lord, I can't do this programme or break my habit on my own," he prayed, kneeling down beside a chair in the lounge. "I am asking You to forgive my sins and come into my life, and please help me to live for You from now on. Amen."

It was a simple prayer, but it was uttered with all the sincerity of a broken human being in the presence of a holy, loving, powerful God.

Matthew then went to his room, rolled into bed, and fell into a satisfied, exhausted sleep almost at once. When he awoke an hour later he discovered that God had heard and answered his plaintive cry from the heart. He knew straight away that something inside him had changed. Life seemed to have taken on a new perspective. He felt that he was possessed, in some inexplicable way, with an inner power he had never experienced before.

Matthew Runcie had become a new creation in Christ Jesus.

Life was busy in the centre and although Matthew told his instructors of his decision to trust in Christ, much to their delight, it was almost a week before he had the time or the inclination to write home to Fraserburgh. Letter writing hadn't been something he had to do often in his life up until then, so it didn't come easily to him. When he did eventually write back to his parents to tell them of his commitment he could have had no idea what that simple letter was to mean to them.

Helen sat with it in her hands casting her eyes over the same page, and the same nine lines in her son's sprawling handwriting, over and over again.

'On Wednesday morning at 5.30 A.M. I gave my life to Jesus,' was what she read. 'I'm trying hard down here to get more involved with the Bible and with Jesus but it is hard but I know that is to be expected on this narrow road...'

The praying Christian mother's hands had begun to shake as she held the letter, and the tears had started to stream from her eyes, as she whispered in a hoarse croak, "I just can't believe this! I just can't believe it!"

She was like the people in the prayer meeting in the Bible. They had been asking God to work a miracle and release Peter from prison but when he came to their door, knocking to get in, they told Rhoda she was mad for telling them he was there!

Like those people, too, however, she would very soon come to accept it, and rejoice in it.

For it was marvellously, miraculously, true!

Chapter 20
# THAT'S GREAT, GOD, BUT...!

It should have been an eagerly anticipated, relaxing occasion.

David and Helen had been invited to a wedding on Saturday 21 st October and Helen's mum and dad had arrived round to the house to see them before they set off. It was hard, though, to look forward to a day out with the worry of the family hanging over their heads. The news from Matthew was fantastic, but the discovery about David, and the overwhelming evidence that Jonathan was also using heroin, had served to dilute their delight. A restraining 'but' bridled any outward, wholehearted expression of their joy.

"We have had tremendous news from Matthew, he has given his life to the Lord," they would tell their Christian friends, "but will you continue to pray that David and Jonathan will do the same."

"ThankYou, Lord, for this wonderful answer to prayer, and for what You are doing in Matthew's life," they would pray, "but please can You, in all Your mighty power and wisdom, do the same for the other two boys?"

Jonathan demonstrated, that Saturday morning, why they felt so fettered.

He had left the sea for a while at that time to pursue a college art course, and was funding his studies by working part-time in a fish factory. This part-time working, part-time studying style of life meant that Jonathan was much worse off financially than when he was at sea, where the work was harder and the hours were longer but the pay was better. His budgetary problems were made even worse by the fact that all those who knew him were aware that he would stop at nothing to obtain money so they took every possible precaution to prevent him from stealing theirs! He was constantly in need of drugs, but constantly short of funds, and it was his persistent plaguing of his mum for money that led to the confrontation.

"I have no money and I need money!" Jonathan roared as he roamed about angrily through the house like a caged lion. "Why will you not give me some, mum?" he pleaded. "I need it to buy materials for my art course."

Helen had heard it all before. She had listened to so many desperate pleas for funds over the previous two or three years that she wasn't going to be hoodwinked by patently paltry excuses. "No, Jonathan, I am not giving you any money. You are working down in the fish factory to fund your art course. That was the agreement," she replied, adamantly. "I won't be handing you any money for I have a fair idea what you would spend it on!"

That firm refusal was too much for Jonathan to take.

He had to come up with the cash from somewhere to buy drugs, and when he realised that he was on a futile mission with his mum, his frustration spilled over. In a split second of blind fury he lifted the kitchen chair that he had been standing beside and threw it. The chair was so heavy and it had been flung with such force that one of its legs punched a hole in the door out into the hall.

Having vented his fury in such dramatic fashion Jonathan then strode to the front door and stormed out through it. He only stopped momentarily to close the door behind him with such venom that every pane of glass in the bungalow shook.

Granda Johnston, who was a man of few words and much

prayer, had been sitting forward during the fracas, leaning on the crook of his walking stick.

"Oh Jonathan, oh Jonathan!" he said softly, shaking his head despondently with his eyes half-closed.

It was hardly the ideal atmosphere from which to leave for a wedding and David and Helen returned home at the earliest possible opportunity that evening. They were never quite sure who, or what, they were going to find in the house after a day away. It could have been worse that day, though.

When his fit of temper subsided Jonathan had climbed in through his brother David's bedroom window and had shut himself off to sulk in his room. At least he was alone. He hadn't a crowd of his cronies in with him, as sometimes happened.

His mum tried to speak to him but it was pointless.

Jonathan was in too foul a frame of mind to exchange pleasantries with anyone.

Helen did, at that time, need to talk to someone outside the immediate family. She felt that she should share her problems and deep concerns with a few of the senior staff, and her closest work colleagues, at the local Primary School where she worked as a lunchtime auxiliary. When she did so, in the week after Jonathan's outburst, she found them extremely sympathetic.

"That must be awful to live with, Helen," some of them commiserated. "We are glad you told us, though. We will do what we can to help you in any way, now that we know. Just feel free to talk to us at any time."

It was reassuring to have such understanding colleagues, and it wouldn't be long until she was back sharing with them again. But it would be about young David next time!

Just over a week later an envelope bearing the logo of their bank, and addressed to Mr. D. Runcie, arrived in the post. Assuming it to be the statement of the joint account she shared with her husband, Helen slit it open.

What a shock!

It was their son David's monthly credit card statement, which she had opened by mistake. And it was almost three thousand pounds in debt!

How could this be? David had a secure job with a major engineering firm in Aberdeen and was supposed to be saving for the future. Where was all his money going?

Although David offered all sorts of farfetched explanations as to why his account was so heavily 'in the red' his parents found them hard to credit. The simple answer to the question of where his money was going was that it was ending up in the pockets of the drug dealers of Fraserburgh and Peterhead.

This was just another problem for David and Helen to take on board, another hurdle to be overcome, another item to be added to an already very lengthy, and lengthening virtually daily, prayer list.

Early November brought a faint glimmer of hope that perhaps things were going to take a turn for the better. Jonathan came home from his art class one afternoon and announced that he was going out the following evening to play football 'with the Solid Rock crowd,' as he called them, 'up in the Academy gym.'

Helen was pleased. If he could build up some sort of a relationship with Ben and the other leaders at The Solid Rock Café who could tell what might happen? Was this the first link in the chain that would draw him to God, the first rung on a ladder to heaven?

Her optimism was to prove short-lived and ill-founded.

At nine-thirty that evening someone phoned from the Accident and Emergency Unit of the local hospital. Jonathan had broken his leg at the football and was in casualty! That was his first and last match with the Solid Rock group. He hadn't had the chance to build up anything even resembling a rapport with them!

What is going to happen next? the hard-pressed parents wondered.

They hadn't long to wait to find out. Crises seemed to be tripping over each other to occur in the Runcie household.

Young David came home from work one day with the news that his employers had arranged for him to go for a special drugs test on Friday 22 nd December. Apparently his line manager had noticed that his attitude and performance had gradually deteriorated since he had been first employed, so he had requested the test.

His appointment was early in the morning of the twenty-second, so David set off from home when it was still pitch dark to allow himself ample time for the forty-mile journey. His parents were both off work that day and were still in bed when he arrived back into the house shortly after seven-thirty. His car had broken down on the road, he said, and a lorry driver had given him a lift back to Fraserburgh.

"Well how very convenient!" was his dad's instinctive reaction, wrongly suspecting that his son was trying to avoid attending for his test. His car *had* actually broken down, as he was to discover later.

"Come on, David!" he said, instantly springing into action. " Give me ten minutes and I will take you to Aberdeen myself!"

It didn't even take ten minutes until they were on the road and as they were pushed for time David the driver set off at a cracking pace. Not only was he still suspicious of young David's very timely 'breakdown,' but he was also annoyed at having to rise so early on his day off when he had been expecting to enjoy a 'lie in.'

There was little conversation in the car. This tension increased during the white-knuckle ride down the road.

They had just passed through the village of Mintlaw, when a traffic policeman stepped out into the middle of the road and signalled for the car to stop. Another delay! This would be more time wasted.

"You have just broken the speed limit in Mintlaw," the constable said, when David rolled down the window. He then proceeded to take down all the particulars he needed to make a prosecution.

"I'm sorry," David apologised, "but we are in a bit of a hurry. My son has an important appointment in Aberdeen, and we don't want to be late."

When he had taken down all the details, and listened to David's excuse, the constable went on, "It's fortunate that we are just on a training exercise. You won't be booked, but this should be a lesson to you."

As they drove on, within the national speed limit, David remarked, "You know you are really jammy, dad."

David the dad had to laugh. His son was right in this instance!

At least the incident seemed to relieve the tension for the remainder of the journey.

It was difficult to enjoy a 'Happy Christmas' with the results of a drugs test that could determine David's future in his job expected in January. And when they did come through the news was not good.

The tests had proved positive and David was facing dismissal.

The young employee was thoroughly sickened by this prospect for he was good at his job, and needed the income it generated. He asked his employers for one last chance and they agreed to give it to him.

The deal was that he would go to the doctor and commence a three-month course of prescription drugs to wean himself off heroin and he would be tested again in six months time. Since his finances also needed some sorting out, young David agreed to allow his mum and dad to help him.

Helen was to control his medication, and his dad was to take charge of his money. He would not even be given the money to put petrol in his car. His dad would do that for him.

Everyone, from his employers through to his close friends and family, were behind him in this last ditch attempt to save his job. Those Christians who loved him were praying fervently that God would give him the strength of will to kick the habit.

David had every incentive to succeed.

He had six months.

Could he do it?

Chapter 21
# CAN I BRING MY WASHING HOME?

Having a son test positive for drugs, and living under the threat of losing his job was a heavy burden for David and Helen to carry with them into a new year.

Before the end of January, though, they were to sustain another blow, but from a different quarter. They never seemed to know where the next staggering punch was going to come from, or when it would be landed into the reeling realm of their lives. This one came under innocent cover, in the form of yet another bank statement.

Helen opened the envelope to discover that her personal account was inexplicably overdrawn. It was most peculiar. She mentioned it to David and he passed it off by observing that she had probably gone 'over the top' at Christmas. His wife usually kept a close check on her spending, though, and she had genuine reservations. Surely she couldn't have been that irresponsible.

A second statement, just two days later, confirmed her worst fears. Her account was now far deeper 'in the red' than it had been before, and she couldn't recall spending anything out of it in the intervening days!

Something was definitely, and seriously amiss. Urgent action was required.

An immediate call to the bank revealed an interesting piece of information. The substantial sum of money, which represented the difference in the two statements, had been withdrawn from the auto teller within the preceding four days. And Helen hardly ever used the 'hole in the wall'!

On the suggestion of the bank clerk to whom she had spoken on the phone Helen went to her handbag as soon as she had replaced the receiver to check on the whereabouts of her bankcard. It was not in its usual place in her wallet.

It was missing.

Someone had stolen her card, found out her PIN, and was clearing out her account.

Who, though, would be doing such a mean thing?

Again Helen had her suspicions.

The bank had suggested that if the card hadn't reappeared in a few days time perhaps they could arrange for her to view the CCTV footage of those using the ATM at the local branch. If it had been used at that machine the person using it would have been caught on camera.

When Helen mentioned the mystery of the strangely unaccounted for card, and the horror of the rifled account, to Jonathan, he said he knew nothing whatsoever about it. He would never do anything like that. How dare she even suggest such a thing!

The promise of an appointment to view the bank's closed circuit TV film provided a useful instrument for putting his still unconvinced mum's hunch to the test. It would also prove the truth of Jonathan's protestations of innocence.

"That's O.K then, Jonathan," she told him, amazing even herself at the show of credulity she was able to effect. "You can come down with me to the bank and have a look at their closed circuit TV footage. You know a lot of the guys around this town and will probably be able to help us identify who *is* actually using my card. I want to see if the film will reveal anything before I turn the whole matter over to the police."

Realizing that he was in an awkward position, and not

having any desire to witness himself robbing his mother, Jonathan confessed that he had been guilty all along. He had no money with which to reimburse her, though. It had all gone on drugs.

This incident led David and Helen to give Jonathan a stern reminder of their policy on the use of drugs in the house. David had been given a last chance to prove that he could kick the habit. If Jonathan didn't beat his addiction, and certainly if he was ever caught using heroin now, he would have to be asked to leave. No excuses would be tolerated, no leniency shown. He was on his 'last legs.'

This ultimatum, plus the fact that he couldn't earn as much money in the fish factory as he could on a fishing boat, helped Jonathan make up his mind on another matter. He told his parents that he was going down to the harbour 'to look for a berth.' He was determined to go to sea again. That way he could make enough to supply his habit, and he would be out of the house seven to ten days at a time. As always, Helen was happier when he was far out in the North Sea working hard. At least he couldn't get up to any mischief out there. He did, though have to come home for the boat to land its catch occasionally, and he had a 'trip off' from time to time.

Then one never knew what was going to happen next.

In early April 2001 Matthew phoned from rehab. He had been moved on to the second stage of his course at a Teen Challenge centre in Wales, and was looking forward to his mum and dad coming down to visit him the next weekend. Matthew had something he wanted his parents to do for him.

"Please, mum," he asked, "could you withdraw some money from my Building Society account and bring it down to me when you are coming?"

"Certainly, son, no problem," Helen replied, thrilled that one third of her family had a bankbook, and money in his account.

What she had described as 'no problem,' turned out to be quite a problem, however. When she went to pick up the savings book from the drawer in her bedroom where it had been put for safekeeping, it wasn't there!

A frantic, but fruitless search ensued. Helen then phoned a Christian girl whom she knew, and who worked for the Building Society. She promised to make some enquiries, and advised Helen to go into her local office the next day to see if they could trace details of the account.

A thorough investigation revealed that a young man, whom the cashier knew to be 'one of the Runcies,' and whom she had presumed to be Matthew, had come in with the book three weeks before and withdrawn four hundred pounds.

Jonathan had struck again!

Matthew rang a few days later to make final plans for his parents visit for the long weekend. He was looking forward to it so much, he said. When he heard that his younger brother had relieved him of most of his funds he was flabbergasted. Nobody understood the compelling urge to obtain money to buy 'gear' any better than him, but it was hard to take in when it affected his own bank account.

"I just can't believe it!" he kept repeating. "I just can't believe it!"

He had to learn to come to terms with it, though, for it was painfully true.

That weekend in Wales was a wonderful blessing to David and Helen. They took Matthew out for the day on the Saturday and his progress, both physical and spiritual, was like a tonic to them. He was looking extremely fit and healthy, and was not afraid to talk about the Lord, about his faith, and about the prayer times he was having with some of the others.

Those were thrilling, inspirational days, hundreds of miles from Fraserburgh.

As they sped northwards on their way home the sunny spiritual high on which they had left Wales seemed to become clouded over with every town or village they either passed by or drove through. With Matthew doing so well their horizon wasn't completely black any more. By the time they had reached the northeast of Scotland it had settled into its usual gloomy shade of grey.

As they drew close to their bungalow home the questions began to arise in their minds.

Would David have kept to the strict schedule that they had all agreed would be best for him?

And what of Jonathan? 'Oh Jonathan, Oh Jonathan!' his granda had exclaimed in soul anguish six months before. When was their youngest son going to hit rock bottom and begin to 'wise up?' What would he be at next?

As usual, they didn't have long to wait to find out.

On the day after they had returned from their visit to Wales, David had gone to work as usual and Helen had set off on a shopping trip to Aberdeen. As he had some matters to clear up at home, David returned to the house about an hour earlier than usual to find Jonathan surrounded by tinfoil, 'chasing the dragon' in his bedroom. Helen and he had always suspected that he was taking drugs in the house but could never prove it. Now he had the evidence, right before his eyes.

David had no option but to put their policy into practice straight away.

"Look, Jonathan, you have been well warned," he began, his severe exterior camouflaging a hurting heart, "you know the score. You will just have to pack up your stuff and go. We can't tolerate this behaviour any longer."

With that he left the room, and Jonathan to his thoughts. There was nothing more to say, and no reply was expected.

When Helen came home later, he had disturbing news for her.

"I've just caught Jonathan using heroin in the house," he informed her, "and I was left with no choice but to tell him to go."

The mother was stunned. Her husband and she had agreed that anyone caught taking drugs would have to go. She recognised that Jonathan could not be given any more chances. What she hadn't ever taken time to seriously contemplate was how she would react if, or when, the crunch actually came.

Now it had arrived.

David was right. He had been left with no choice.

Longsuffering had been stretched out very long.

Now the time had come for the rules to be enforced.

Helen assured her husband of her full support, and then hurried upstairs to the bedroom where Jonathan was throwing a few clothes and a CD or two rather disconsolately into a holdall. All she wanted to do was give him a big hug.

Jonathan put his arm around his mum. They were both upset.

"Now you see what he has done. He has put me out!" Jonathan exclaimed angrily, hoping to make the most of his mum's breaking heart, by placing the blame for his eviction on his dad.

"Don't blame your dad," Helen replied, trying to be brave. "You know, Jonathan, that was what we had decided, and you were well warned. Anybody caught using drugs would have to go."

Tearing herself away from her crestfallen son Helen went back downstairs to prepare the evening meal.

She was peeling potatoes, and her tears were dripping into the basin, when Jonathan appeared behind her with his holdall in his hand. He had come to say goodbye.

When she turned to face him, he saw that she was crying and offered a chilling rebuke. "Oh mum, stop that greetin'," he growled sarcastically. "You have had so much hassle with me you will probably be glad to see the end of me anyway. 'Bye."

That only made Helen worse.

Jonathan didn't even wait to see his mum collapse into floods of tears, though. He merely steeled himself, turned abruptly, and walked straight out of the house. The front door closed after him.

He was gone.

It was hard, but somewhat alleviated by the fact that Jonathan came back less than two hours later with a welcome item of news, and a simple request.

His news was that he had found a flat to rent, and his request tugged at his mum's tangled heartstrings, yet again.

"The old washing machine in this place I am going to doesn't work," he said. "So I was wondering if I could bring my washing home?"

Helen just wanted to say, 'Yes certainly, son, no problem. Bring it home and I'll do it for you.' But she couldn't.

This was the time for discipline, both for her son, and herself.

Her measured response to her son's question showed both a leniency engendered by love and an admirable sense of control. "Yes, Jonathan, you can bring your washing home," she informed him, "on two conditions. The first is that either your dad and I are in the house when you come, and the second is that you actually do the washing yourself."

"That's fair enough," her son agreed.

It was then time for David, the dad, whom Jonathan had somehow seen as the villain of the piece, to have his say. "We just want you to understand, Jonathan, that it is not our intention to put you out of this house forever. When you have mended your ways, and are off drugs, you will always be welcome back here," he told him.

"Thanks, dad," Jonathan replied, obviously grateful.

With Jonathan coming back and forward to do his washing, and with the door having been left open for him to return, subject to certain conditions, contact would not be completely cut off.

Mum and dad were both glad of that.

Chapter 22
# OUT OF THE DEEP

It was Thursday, July 19 th 2001.

Jonathan had been at sea for two days on the fishing boat 'Vertrauen.' The early days of any trip were always harrowing for addicts like him. It was particularly hard going on the 'Vertrauen' too for she was a larger boat and the nets were hauled more often than on some of the smaller vessels. The work was endless and often exhausting and Jonathan's body was constantly crying out for a 'fix' to keep it going, but drug taking aboard the boats was prohibited. Apart from the rules of the sea, it was virtually impossible anyway because by that time Jonathan had used up all his available funds to satisfy his habit when ashore.

The sun shone out across a still shimmering sea that day. The fine weather and pleasant conditions hadn't done anything to improve Jonathan's mixed-up mood or sense of physical well-being, though. He had come to depend on heroin for his feel-good-factor, and nothing else.

They had a problem that afternoon, but it was one that was usually easily overcome. The portside net had snagged on the bottom. The crew spent almost two hours trying to haul it in. This was strange. Normally a snagged net would pull free in a very short space of time and the boat would be on its way again.

The net did eventually break loose of whatever was holding it but the crew were unable to haul it aboard. It came halfway, then stopped. The engine powering the hydraulics had cut out. The skipper went below to try and discover what the problem was.

The deckhands welcomed the break. They stood around on the sunlit deck, smoking. It wouldn't be long until the nets would be back in the water and the perpetual procedure of nets out, nets in, catch out, nets out, nets in… would start all over again. Better make the best of the rest when they had the chance.

When the skipper reappeared on deck his face was deathly pale. He looked like someone in shock.

Staring almost blankly across at where the other three members of his crew were standing, two of them nonchalantly flicking cigarette ash over the side, he growled just three words in a hoarse whisper.

"The boat's sinking!" was his blunt message.

Within seconds the sunny day, laissez-faire atmosphere on deck vanished, melting away like early morning mist. The languid 'Vertrauen' became transformed into a hive of anxious activity.

Each man reacted to the alarming news in a different way. Jonathan's impulse was to go and take a look for himself, and what he found filled him with horror. There was seawater sloshing about gently down below.

The men tried to operate the pumps but to no effect. It was a losing battle.

Realizing that they were in grave danger the skipper immediately sent out a Mayday message. 'Boat taking water. In urgent need of helicopter with a pump,' was the earnest appeal over the airwaves.

Jonathan went out on deck to see what was happening, then went back below. It was frightening. Anything that had been lying around and was light enough to float was floating around in water a few feet deep. He checked the level of the water on the rungs of the ladder and was convinced that it had risen since his last visit below fifteen minutes before.

There was nothing to do now but wait. On rejoining the others Jonathan was pleased to see that help was at hand. A standby ship for the oilrigs had responded immediately to the skipper's distress call, and was standing off.

Jonathan went down to the galley to see if he could find something to eat before everything became saturated with seawater, and before it was time to leave the vessel. There was little else to do. The starboard net hung idle over its drum. The other one trailed out astern, its winding gear not working. Their only chance of ever being used again would be if the 'Vertrauen' could be saved. That was looking increasingly unlikely.

The most chilling moment came when the engines spluttered, then stopped.

An eerie silence crept over the motionless vessel. She seemed to sit solidly in the sea. There was no throb of engines, no lapping water, no chatter amongst the crew. Even the surrounding seagulls seemed to sense the seriousness of the situation and stopped their incessant shrieking.

It was weird. Uncanny.

A sunny day, a calm sea and a silently sinking boat.

The skipper spoke out of the wheelhouse to the remainder of the crew who were standing around in the galley, and said, "Look guys, we're going to have to get off this boat. She's going down. I have asked the standby ship to dispatch its FRC (fast rescue craft) to fetch us."

The crew ran up on deck. They had been expecting that message to come sooner or later. It seemed as though it were going to be sooner. Jonathan noticed that the stern of the boat had now sunk deeper into the water and the deck had taken on a decided tilt. The skipper was right. She was going down. The FRC would be welcome anytime.

Meanwhile, as he looked around Jonathan noticed that although the 'Vertrauen' was fully equipped with life jackets, none of the men on board was wearing one. As there was no sign of the rescue craft approaching a sense of dread fell like a heavy shadow over the boat. Realising that they were likely to end up in the water Jonathan made one final foray below to retrieve the life jackets.

It wasn't easy. The water was up to his knees, but that was neither the sole nor most difficult problem. This lay in the fact that the life jackets were designed to inflate when coming into contact with water, and had inflated then floated up into the galley. Retrieving folded life jackets would have been dangerous enough in the rising flood on board, but bringing them out on deck inflated, proved a mammoth task. They were now so large and they had to be transported from the galley to the deck, up an awkward stairway and then through the congested wheelhouse. The toggles on the jackets seemed to keep catching on everything!

The youngest crewmember on board managed to bring four jackets out on deck, one for each of them, but as it turned out they were not needed.

The fast rescue craft had arrived alongside and all four members of the ill-fated fishing boat's crew climbed across into it, with the skipper last to step over her side. The crew were glad to get off for by that time they could physically feel the boat slipping beneath the waves in a freshening wind.

The FRC powered away at speed and then slowed to a purring stop at a safe distance. This allowed the men who had pulled thousands of kilos of fish aboard the 'Vertrauen' to witness her last moments.

As the stern sank slowly into the North Sea the bow pointed upward like an accusing finger at the blue sky. She seemed reluctant to leave the surface over which she had sailed smoothly and battled bravely for many years.

When the end did come it was gradual, and graceful. The Vertrauen just slipped slowly below the surface. The point of her bow lingered for a few last seconds as though to bid all those who had laboured to earn a living on her a final farewell.

Then she was gone.

All of a sudden there was nothing left except a few odd bits of flotsam that had escaped from the deck, stubbornly refusing to go down with her. They bobbed about on the remaining ripples of her disappearance.

These ripples were soon gone too.

The sea had turned frighteningly empty again.

It was as though the Vertrauen had never existed.

There was nothing left to do but turn away, set the FRC to full throttle and return to the standby ship.

An hour later a helicopter came whirring overheard and the rescued crew were winched up into it with a line. Soon they would be back ashore, days earlier than they had ever anticipated, and in a most unexpected way.

When the helicopter landed on the Links, a large open space on the edge of Fraserburgh, there was great excitement. News of the sinking of the 'Vertrauen' had reached the fishing community ashore and a small crowd had gathered to greet the incoming helicopter.

The families of the other crewmembers were there to meet them. There were subdued scenes of thankfulness. Tears and hugs were the order of the day. Husbands, fathers and sons had been rescued from what could have been a watery grave.

But there was nobody there to meet Jonathan.

The lad who had just been rescued from a sinking boat had to return to a cheerless flat on his own.

The son who had been asked to leave home for persistent drug abuse now found himself very much alone in the world.

And it hurt. Badly.

Chapter 23
# BE STILL, MY SOUL

Decision day for David junior came in late August.

His six-month probation period had come to an end. He was summoned to attend for another drugs test.

This proved positive.

Everybody who had any impact whatsoever on David's life, be they parents, employers, fiancée or friends, had been extremely supportive of him in the early months of the year. They so much wanted to see him dispense with the drugs, and live a 'normal' life. He couldn't do it, though. The heroin habit had such a hold on him that he just couldn't shake himself free of it.

David had blown his second chance.

And there wasn't going to be a third.

His employers had made it clear to him that if he tested positive again he would be dismissed. Having given him fair warning they had no choice but to ask him to leave immediately they were informed of the test result.

The next time he met his fiancée he had a double confession to make. He was still on drugs and had lost his job. The patient young woman could take no more. She had always been hoping for a brighter day but the days seemed to be becoming nothing but bleaker.

His dad's predictions of almost a year before were coming true. David was in the process of losing all the promising prospects in his life, 'for the sake of that rubbish.' He was now faced with massive problems, and all of them of his own making.

There was a three thousand pound deficit in his Visa account still to be settled, despite his dad's attempts to monitor his money, and he had entered into an agreement to purchase a house. The mortgage repayments on this new property were due to be taken up in October.

His parents, who had been through so much, stepped in again to succour where they could and be firm where they should.

They contacted the solicitors in Aberdeen and asked them to put David's house on the market again. He wouldn't need it now. They then advised David to contact Ben Ritchie down in the Solid Rock Café. Ben offered valuable assistance in two ways, one immediate and practical, the other future and both physical and spiritual.

Firstly he arranged a job for David in Whitelink Seafoods, the fish factory in which he worked. The money earned from this employment would allow David to start clearing off his outstanding debts. Ben also helped him to complete and send off an application form for Teen Challenge.

David had come to the end of his tether. He had arrived at a position where everything looked hopeless and pointless. If attending Teen Challenge could help him sort out the mess his life was in, then he would go there. Nothing could be worse, he reckoned, than his present woebegone situation.

That September was to become the most miserable month in young David Runcie's life. He hated the fish factory. It was hard, physical work in a cold, damp environment. The dramatic deterioration in his circumstances had led to him losing weight and also becoming terribly depressed. The once strong, healthy, positive young Christian now weighed just over eight stones. He didn't want to get up in the morning, and he didn't want to go down to the fish factory. In fact he didn't want to do anything only end it all.

There were times when he felt suicidal. If I could just pluck up the courage to jump into the harbour, he told himself, that would put an end to this miserable existence...

Ben, his mentor, understood him, though. This was the vision which had led Victor and he to establish the Solid Rock Café. They wanted to help lads like David make it through. Teen Challenge had introduced a new condition of acceptance to their course. Prospective students had to phone in to the centre in Keighley every day to prove that they were serious about their application. They had to convince the management that they meant business before they could be taken.

All throughout that month of misery Ben made sure that David came to his office at some time of the day and made his phone call. This kept his application alive at Teen Challenge.

Although Ben was keen to see him go to rehab, and so were his parents, David didn't really care by then whether he went or not. All he wanted to do was run away. It was such a great temptation, just to get up and go somewhere different or do something desperate, that he tried it one day.

Morning break time came in the factory and David was feeling particularly rotten. He went to the toilet, and instead of returning to his workstation he made sure that nobody was watching, and walked out. His disappearance caused Ben, and then his parents when they were informed, some concern. They all knew his unstable mental state. Where could he be? What would he do?

David and Helen contacted everyone they knew who they thought might be able to help. One of their first calls was to David's friends Alexander and Lisa West. They knew their son often resorted to that caring couple's house when feeling down. Although many of David's former friends had deserted him in his dilemma, Alexander and Lisa hadn't. David had told his parents once how much he valued their friendship, especially after the night they had told him, "No matter what happens, David, you can depend on us. We will always be there for you."

He wasn't at Alexander and Lisa's house that day, though.

It was almost nine o'clock in the evening when he reappeared at home, much to his mum and dad's delight. Helen had become so worried that when she saw him again, still alive, neither she nor her husband had troubled to ask him where he had been. Even if they had they probably wouldn't have been told the truth anyway.

Their son had spent the day at a dealer's house, trying in vain to achieve some sort of physical satisfaction or mental peace.

In addition to her genuine concern about David's obviously worsening condition, the house in Aberdeen, which would become his parent's responsibility if unsold, caused Helen untold anguish that September. She prayed a lot, shared often with compassionate Christian friends, and made occasional anxious phone calls to Aberdeen.

Her husband, the other David in her life, had, by way of contrast, an unusual experience early in the month. This allowed him to cope more positively with yet another potentially perplexing situation.

He was driving along between calls at work, with Classic FM playing on the radio. It wasn't that he was listening particularly to what was being played but as a musician he always found it comforting to have music as a backdrop to his busy life.

Suddenly a piece was played which cried out for his undivided attention. The music that had been floating over him in a soothing stream, enhancing his environment but little else, became, at that moment, markedly more meaningful.

A rich voice had just begun to sing,

'Be still, my soul, the Lord is on thy side,
Bear patiently the cross of grief or pain,
Leave to thy God to order and provide,
In every change He faithful will remain.
Be still, my soul, thy best, thy heavenly Friend
Through thorny ways leads to a joyful end.'

David was listening intently to every word as the second verse began. He felt that hymn, halfway through an otherwise secular programme, had been sent straight from God for him. The words seemed to fill the car as they went on,

'Be still, my soul, thy God doth undertake
To guide the future as He has the past,
Thy hope, thy confidence let nothing shake,
All now mysterious shall be bright at last.
Be still, my soul, the winds and waves still know,
His voice who ruled them while He dwelt below.'

The singer was moving on into the final verse, but David's mind was still firmly implanted in verse two. The thought that God had undertaken to guide the future as He had guided the past gripped him. The God who had seen Matthew to rehab, could do the same for David. And who knows, even for Jonathan. What seemed a mystery and a mess at the minute could be, and would be, resolved, and revealed at last. He was sure of that. God had told him so, very definitely, that day. David just continued to join Helen in praying that it would be soon.

They had to wait until Wednesday 3 rd October for the answers to their passionate prayers of the previous month, but when they came, they came all at once in a superabundance of blessing.

Helen picked up the mail in the hall at ten past nine, and anxiously opened an official looking envelope. It was to tell them that David's house had been sold. "Oh thank You Lord!" she exclaimed in an instinctive expression of praise and adoration.

"I just can't believe this!" she continued, moving through into the kitchen, envelope in one hand, letter in the other.

"Well I can," her husband replied softly. His normally easy-going nature led to his being, as a general rule, less exuberant than his wife about most matters. Now however, his calm though nonetheless appreciative approach to such glad tidings came, not from his personality, but from a confidence in the power of God. This he had gleaned though a hymn heard in the car. "That is what I expected. Isn't that what we have all been praying so hard about for the last six weeks or so?"

The relieved and thankful couple were still discussing the impact of the letter when the telephone rang at nine twenty-five.

Helen went to answer it.

"Is that Mrs. Runcie?" the voice enquired. "How are things?" It was one of the senior leaders at Teen Challenge.

"I'm just standing here with tears running down my face," Helen burst out in her excitement. " We are praising God for a wonderful answer to prayer. A letter has just arrived to say that David's house in Aberdeen has been sold! At least that will be less mental and emotional baggage for him to take with him to Teen Challenge when you can hopefully find a place for him down there."

"Well that's just what we are ringing to say, Mrs. Runcie," the leader went on. "A place has become available for David and he can start with us tomorrow if you can get him down!"

Helen was absolutely overjoyed, and even David had to admit that this was bordering on the unbelievable. Not only was God's power fantastic but His timing was also perfect.

Meanwhile down in Whitelink Seafoods David had begun another dreary day. Just before ten o'clock Ben came looking for him. "David, could I see you in my office?" he said, looking unusually stern.

What have I done now? the young employee wondered as he followed along a few steps behind his friend and mentor. Am I about to get sacked for coming in late, or skiving off early? Or maybe it's about that row I had the other day...

When they reached the solitude of the office the Ben's face broke into a big smile. He had decided to make the lad sweat a minute or two, just for the fun of it.

"Your mum has just been on phone," he began, "and she asked me to tell you a couple of things. Your house has been sold, and Teen Challenge want you down to start the programme tomorrow. Your dad is taking the day off to drive you there. Are you O.K. to go?"

"Yes, that will be all right," David replied. Anything, he reckoned, would be an improvement on his present position and condition.

"We can release you at any time then if you have preparations to make," Ben continued to explain. "You can finish out the day if you like, or go at lunch time, or even at the morning break."

"I'll just tidy up my stuff now, and go at the morning break," David told him.

He did, too, and this time it was to be for good.

A second Runcie son was on his way to Teen Challenge.

Chapter 24
# IT'S GREAT TO BE HOME!

"You'll hear the full story of the 'Vertrauen' from him when he comes in," Helen told Steve Worth, a Christian friend from Aberdeen. Steve had worked in Fraserburgh for some time, and when there had attended Bethesda Evangelical Church. He had come to know the Runcie family well during those days, and had called for a cup of tea and a chat during a visit back to the 'Broch' during November 2001.

Steve had been fascinated to hear of Jonathan's rescue from the sinking fishing-boat during the previous summer. It would be interesting to hear his first-hand account of it sometime, he thought.

Later that night Jonathan arrived up at the bungalow, which had once been his home, with a pile of clothes to be washed, all bundled into a black polythene bag.

When he had finished his washing Jonathan joined Steve and his mum and dad who were sitting chatting around the table. He sat down on a chair beside Helen and began to join in the conversation. His mum put her arm around him and said, "I'll just give you a cuddle like I used to do when you were a little boy."

Jonathan wasn't a little boy then, though. He was a working man of twenty. Normally he would not have been particularly pleased to have his mum fussing over him, but he didn't seem to mind that evening.

He was glad to feel the comfort of someone who cared

for him, touching him. It was so reassuring. It was obvious to all three adults watching him, and listening to him, however, that Jonathan hadn't come straight to his parents' house with his washing when he came ashore. He must have stopped off somewhere to buy, and use, some 'gear' for he was already 'dipping.' His eyes were closing and his head was falling forward involuntarily. Perhaps this was a second reason why he was happy to allow his mum to sit with her arm around him.

Steve recognised that Jonathan had been using heroin but he was still keen to hear the story of the summer sinking in the North Sea from a survivor. If he could persuade Jonathan to tell the story it would fulfil a dual function. In addition to satisfying his desire to hear a real-life sea saga it would also help to keep the story-teller focused on the here and now.

"Your mum and dad have been telling me about your boat sinking back in July, Jonathan," he said, introducing the subject. "I would like to hear all about it. Why did she go down on a calm day? Were you in any danger of being lost? What exactly happened?"

Steve's patent enthusiasm to hear a good sea yarn proved infectious and Jonathan began with a will. He recounted the problem of the snagged net, the horror of the skipper's discovery, and his struggle with the already inflated life jackets. As he continued the story Steve would interrupt him now and then to ask a question to clarify a point, and so they went on. Jonathan's account of the 'Vertrauen's' fated final moments was quite graphic, as he described how she disappeared slowly, stern-first into the sea.

David and Helen were mesmerised to hear the story in such detail, too. They had heard snippets of it from time to time in different contexts but never the entire tale from beginning to end. They were all engrossed in it, but when

Jonathan came to describing the helicopter flight back to Fraserburgh he had a heart-rending revelation to make.

When he came to the landing at the Links, and the reception the other three crew members were accorded, Jonathan turned round to his mum, looked her straight in the eye, and declared, "You know I felt it badly that day when there was nobody there to meet me. It really, really hurt."

This admission was made without even a hint of malice. It sounded rather as though it came from the hurt heart of that little boy his mum had been telling him about. And by the time he was finished his wasn't the only heart that was hurt.

Helen struggled to hold back the tears.

Although Jonathan had already been told, she felt that she needed to explain, for Steve's sake if nothing else, why there had been nobody there to meet him that lonely day. "You know, Jonathan, we would have been there with all the rest to pick you up that day, if we had been here, but we were on holiday at the time. We were in Greece and I suppose the men at the harbour didn't know who else to contact."

"I understand that, mum," Jonathan conceded. "But it was still hard."

On his next trip home the young fisherman arrived as usual to visit his private launderette. Noticing that it was almost eleven o'clock his mum said to him, "Have you finished all you need to do here, Jonathan? For if you have I will take you home in the car."

Jonathan looked rather abashed for a moment. "Mum, I wonder if it would be OK if I stayed here for the night?" he asked. "I have left the key to my flat on the boat and I won't be able to get it until the morning."

Helen's maternal instincts were stirred. She realised that he was finding it difficult to look after himself in the flat so she said, "Well, OK But just for the night remember."

Next morning Jonathan was away and they didn't see him again until he returned after another trip.

This time he turned up late on a Friday afternoon, and when he had finished his washing he had another request to make. "Do you think I could stay over the weekend?" he enquired, contritely. "It is so lonely and cold in my flat. I have no heat these cold nights for I haven't paid my last bill. It was great that other night I slept back in my own bed. I promise to be no bother and it will only be for a night or two. We are out again first thing on Monday morning."

"We'll see," his mum told him, playing for time. Her natural reaction would be to say, 'Yes certainly son, no problem,' but common sense told her, 'Rules are rules, and if you give in on this one, where do you stop?'

"I will ask your dad, and see what he says," was the most information she could volunteer in the meantime.

When her husband and she discussed it when David came in they decided to let Jonathan stay the weekend on a trial basis. It was only if he 'behaved himself, and didn't bring any of that rubbish into the house.'

Probably recognising that he was on a kind of probation Jonathan behaved impeccably over the weekend. It was so pleasant to have him back in the house again, and in such an agreeable mood, that his mum and dad spoke to him before he set out for the harbour on Monday morning.

"We want you to make up your mind when away at sea," they told him. "We are willing to have you back in the house for good, but only if you are prepared to try and behave yourself and put all this nonsense behind you."

"Thanks, mum and dad," Jonathan replied, gratefully. He could have given them his answer there and then, but it wasn't expected until he returned, so he would, to use their expression, 'make up his mind when away at sea.'

When he came ashore again the following weekend Jonathan went straight home and told his parents that he had thought about their offer when away, and that he was taking them up on it. What was more he even promised to be 'no trouble' and 'as helpful as he could.'

It all sounded wonderful.

And it was, too. For about six or eight weeks.

David and Helen could hardly believe that the Jonathan who had come home to them was the same person they had been forced to ask to leave earlier on in the year. He was agreeable, accommodating, and above all appreciative. After returning to live at home he would tell his mum, at least two or three times every day, "It's great to be home! You have no idea what it means to me to be back here. Just to have a warm bed to sleep in and some decent food to eat…"

His mum and dad were delighted to have him back as well. A facet of family life had been restored to them With Matthew and David both away at Teen Challenge it was good to have Jonathan coming in and out. Perhaps his nine months in exile had taught him a lesson.

It would be great to think that it had.

But sadly it hadn't.

By the end of December things had begun to change.

The Christmas break was to prove a big test for Jonathan. The boats were not out over the holiday period and then for the first week of January owing to bad weather. When the fishermen weren't out fishing they didn't get paid and the deckhand, who had been trying to be ever so good, began to run short of funds, and consequently of patience.

Although he was clever enough not to use heroin in the house now, David and Helen knew that he was using it out somewhere else. A lack of money spelt desperation for the addict who, despite all the promises and resolutions, was held in apparently unbreakable chains by his habit, so he came to his mum one day begging for money.

"Could you lend me some money for cigarettes, mum?" he pleaded. "I will pay you back when the boat goes out again."

"No, Jonathan, I won't," Helen told him firmly. "You may just wait until you are back at work and have made something for yourself."

That was on a Thursday. On the next day, Friday 11 th January 2002, David and Helen were due to return to the choir practice at Bethesda Evangelical Church. Helen always looked forward to the resumption of the choir practices in the New Year for it meant the beginning of another year of praise, of opportunity and of challenge.

It was difficult to anticipate a pleasant evening catching up on the news with all their friends, and tackling some new pieces, that day though. Jonathan, who had been so agreeable and appreciative six weeks before, had now turned both agitated and aggressive. He was stomping around the house muttering under his breath, a permanent scowl on his face. It was as though something was about to explode inside him any minute. He had become like a volcano, just about to erupt.

After one surly exchange with his mum, she confronted him about his attitude. "You have been using that rubbish again!" she declared.

"No, I haven't!" Jonathan was quick to issue a categorical denial of what to his mum, who had become both unwittingly and unwillingly an expert in these matters, was clearly unmistakeable.

An argument ensued and when David heard his wife shout in evident frustration, "There you go, spoiling my night again!" he reckoned that it was high time he intervened.

Finding his angry son, David caught him by the shoulders and marched him to the mirror in the hall. "Open your eyes and take a good look at yourself in that mirror, Jonathan!" he urged. "What do you see? Straggly hair and sallow, pasty skin. A mouthful of broken, rotten teeth! And what do you think has made you like that? It's all that rubbish you have been pumping into yourself!"

When Dad had finished with him, Jonathan was crying. He met Helen as he fled in the direction of the bathroom. He looked at her again full in the face. This time though he didn't look like a letdown child. His countenance now bore all the anguish of a confused, angry adult.

"Do you think I like looking like this?" he screamed at her. "Do you honestly think I can help the way I am? Well I can't! I can't! I can't!"

Recognising that this was the first time Jonathan had even admitted that he had a problem, Helen decided to follow it up with what she considered good advice. "You could always do what the other two have done," she counselled. "You could apply to…"

"No!" Jonathan interrupted her abruptly. He was furious by then. " There is no way that I will be doing what the other two have done! Going to that place is like signing yourself into jail! They just brainwash you there! I'll show you that I can handle this myself!"

That was his parting shot. The bathroom door was slammed in the face of his mother who had been shadowing him as he stormed around.

The subject was closed.

Jonathan believed that he could handle his problem himself.

But could he?

He had been so thrilled to be back home.

How long, though, was he going to be able to stay?

Would he have to be told to go again?

Chapter 25
# DICING WITH DEATH

It was only a matter of time until the crucial decision would have to be taken again in relation to Jonathan. His attitude when at home was becoming increasingly aggressive, his behaviour more withdrawn, and his drug problem certainly hadn't gone away. David and Helen knew that the crunch was coming. It would be the same with Jonathan as it had been with the others, indeed as it had been with him already.

They never knew how or when it would occur.

The only thing of which they could be absolutely certain was that it would.

In the meantime, though, God chose to prepare them for the crisis to come by letting them live on the top of the Mountain of Praise and Thanksgiving for a few weeks. The air was exhilarating up there, and the view breathtaking. It allowed them a period of spiritual refreshing, and a look at the bigger picture. Whatever their heartaches as they struggled through the Valley of Problems and Trials, when they reached that summit they could see that God was still in control.

He *was* hearing their heartfelt cries.

And He *was* answering their persistent prayers, and those of an entire battalion of prayer warriors, marching behind them.

At the end of February 2002, they heard some thrilling news.

David junior phoned from Teen Challenge to tell them that he had rededicated his life to the Lord. This was the son whom they had never suspected of being involved in drugs because of his apparent involvement as a Christian, and who had then been such a surprise and disappointment to them.

Now he was able to testify clearly to his parents that God had helped him conquer his addiction, and that he had vowed to serve Him for the rest of his life.

What an incentive to keep going, keep praying, and keep praising!

Helen went around singing during early March, especially when Jonathan was somewhere out in the North Sea. With two-thirds of her family now living for the Lord she could almost afford to be happy. When the remaining third wasn't about she didn't have to contend with his strident demands or unpredictable mood swings.

With the boats having to return to port to unload their catch, though, Jonathan was still obliged to make the occasional visit ashore. It was then, when he had money in his pocket, either his own or somebody else's, that the problems began.

And Good Friday, 29 th March 2002, was the start of one of those weekends…

David and Helen had been down to the choir practice in the church and had returned home, pleasantly tired. They were relaxing together over supper, before retiring for the night, when the phone rang.

When Helen went to answer it an unfamiliar man's voice enquired, "Is that Mrs. Runcie?" On being assured that it was the caller continued, "This is the police. We are ringing from Fraserburgh Hospital. We have one of your sons here, possibly David."

"Oh no, it couldn't be David!" Helen interrupted involuntarily. "It's Jonathan."

"Well whoever it is," the officer went on, not sounding

entirely convinced, "he has fallen into the harbour. He's O.K. but could you come up and bring him some dry clothes?"

Even though it was nearly midnight David and Helen had to revert from relaxed to active mode, and when they had collected some dry clothes for Jonathan, they drove up to the Hospital.

Two policemen met them just inside the door. One of the officers then showed the hard-pressed parents a credit card they had found in Jonathan's possession.

The name on it was David Runcie. It was his father's card, and he hadn't yet missed it. David was stunned, and felt rather stupid. How could he have been so careless? How or when had Jonathan ever been able to nick that card? Who could blame the puzzled policemen for assuming that the young man they had been summoned to the harbour to find unconscious on the quay was called David?

David and Helen were taken through to the Accident and Emergency unit where they expected to find Jonathan sitting up waiting to change into the dry clothes they had brought.

It came as a jarring shock to discover him stretched out, wrapped up in a tinfoil blanket. His face was colourless and expressionless. He was muttering incoherently. Helen went to take his hand in hers and found it cold to the touch.

His breathing was laboured, coming in short gasps.

As they stood gazing at the sorry figure of their son, who could easily have drowned, a doctor came along.

He opened his hand to reveal three pills. "We found these in his pocket and can only assume that he has taken the rest as part of a crazy cocktail of drugs," he said.

His diagnosis was spot on. David and Helen were later to discover that Jonathan had gone to a dealer that evening and bought one hundred pounds worth of mixed drugs. He had taken the lot except for the three pills in the doctor's hand.

Dad's credit card can come in handy when such 'vital' and expensive purchases have to be made!

"I'm sorry," the doctor went on to inform them, "but we do not have the facilities to treat him here. We have called for an ambulance to take him to the Royal Infirmary in Aberdeen."

Jonathan's parents had only been by his side for about ten minutes when the ambulance arrived. David helped one of the paramedics carry him out into it. The patient who had seemed so comatose when in the hospital seemed to revive when moved out into the cold night air, and began fighting and kicking. He was safely transferred into the ambulance and it sped away.

David and Helen watched as its lights disappeared off into the darkness, but decided not to follow it. Aberdeen was forty miles away, it was then nearly one o'clock in the morning, and when Jonathan arrived at the Royal Infirmary there would be tests to be carried out and treatment to be started.

They would go home and pray. Then ring in the morning.

When Helen rang the hospital the next day the message was that Jonathan was making progress but it would be the Sunday at least before he would be discharged. It would take some time for his body to recover from its drug-induced dip in the harbour the previous night.

The phone rang later that evening. It had come to the stage that David and Helen almost dreaded picking up the receiver, wondering what would be coming next. This time it was David's turn.

"Hi dad! It's Jonathan," the husky voice at the other end began. "Do you know where I'm at?"

"Aye well do I know where you're at, Jonathan," his dad replied, wryly. "I helped you out into the ambulance last night though you didn't know an awful lot about what was going on."

"Can you come down tomorrow afternoon to pick me up?" was the son's next question. "They tell me I'm getting home tomorrow."

"O.K. son. No problem. We'll be there," his dad assured him. His mum then had a chat with him, and she was happy to hear him sounding sensible. He had been completely 'out of it' the night before, and that had worried her.

When they arrived into the Royal Infirmary on the Sunday afternoon to take Jonathan home they found him most annoyed. The medical staff had informed him that he was not to be discharged until the following day.

David made enquiries as to why this should be and was informed that they reckoned it would be best to have Jonathan assessed by a psychiatrist. This was apparently recommended procedure in cases where the patient had been rescued from drowning when alone. They had to establish if Jonathan had jumped, rather than fallen into the harbour. Could this have been a suicide attempt?

Although Jonathan told them that he had just been 'larking about' and fallen in, they weren't prepared to take his word for it. He had to be seen by 'an expert,' and had to remain in hospital another night, despite his protestations.

Jonathan was a very subdued young man when his dad went to bring him home that Easter Monday afternoon. David had to initiate most of the conversation and used the opportunity to challenge his son about his future.

"What are you going to do now, Jonathan?" he asked, pointedly.

"I don't really know. In fact I hadn't really thought about it," was the first non-committal answer he received.

"Well, I think you had better think about it. And seriously, too," his dad went on to caution. "You had a close call last year when your boat sank. This time you could have died from drowning. Or hypothermia. Or a drugs overdose. You are dicing with death, Jonathan. And if you go on like this you are going to end up dead. No question about it."

There was a brief silence in the car. It was the kind of silence that can almost be felt, thick and heavy, just waiting for something to be said or done to carve it open.

Jonathan broke it eventually.

"I suppose I had better fill in the papers for Teen Challenge," he croaked, in a barely audible whisper.

He had come to that critical point where he realized that no matter how hard he tried, his problem was far and away beyond his ability to solve.

Despite his ranting and raving to the contrary, Jonathan couldn't 'handle this' himself.

He desperately needed help.

And he needed it soon.

Chapter 26
# SUMMONED AS A WITNESS

It could prove costly to stand up and be counted.

Young David, now seeking to live an effective Christian life at Teen Challenge was summoned to attend the High Court in Stonehaven, south of Aberdeen, as a witness. A drug dealer had been apprehended by the police, and as David's name had been found on a scrap of paper in his house, he was summoned to attend the trial to be held on Monday and Tuesday 8 - 9 th April 2002.

When he, as a Christian, decided to testify against this dealer, he was allowed home from Teen Challenge for the weekend, and for the duration of the trial. However, late on Friday afternoon Helen received a phone call from the Sheriff Clerk's office in Stonehaven. This was to let David know that owing to a busy day planned for the court on Monday he would not now be called upon until the second day of the trial, which was Tuesday. By this time David was already on his way home.

This left David and his parents in a dilemma.

It also placed Jonathan in a precarious position.

The local dealers weren't to know that David was at home, provided he didn't move out of the house, but they did know where Jonathan was. And they used that knowledge to pressurise him to try to persuade David to change his statement.

Jonathan had just come home from hospital on Easter

Monday and a few days later had completed the application form for Teen Challenge. Although he may not have been altogether one hundred per cent enthusiastic about this he had at least filled it up and sent it off. There would be a waiting time of four to six weeks before he was faced with a final decision.

When the local dealers heard that David had agreed to testify against their associate in custody they began to lean on Jonathan once again.

It would create problems if those guys knew that David was at home, or if they ever found Jonathan alone.

So what should they do?

David wouldn't be required in court until Tuesday.

How, or where, then should they spend Monday?

There seemed to be only one sensible answer.

It was, clear out. Go away for the day. Leave Fraserbugh far behind.

David took a day off work, and as Helen was already still on holiday at the end of the Easter vacation, they set off early in the morning for Inverness, one hundred miles away.

They stopped in Elgin for lunch and then drove on to Inverness where they went ten-pin bowling. David and Helen were pleased to be able to share a day out with their two sons and they in turn were happy to be together again. The three boys had always been very close and Jonathan missed the company of his two older brothers since they had both gone away. And in the current set of circumstances they all felt more relaxed far away from Fraserburgh.

The family group was just finishing their rather hilarious game of ten-pin bowls when David had a call on his mobile phone from Bet, his secretary. The Sheriff Clerk from Stonehaven, on finding the phone at the Runcie home repeatedly unanswered, had called David's office with a message. He wanted to let both Davids, one the potential witness and the other his dad, who doubled as his driver and bodyguard, know that David the younger would not be required to attend court the following day. The accused had pleaded guilty to all charges and so it would be unnecessary to call any witnesses.

This was good news for the Runcies on the run for two reasons.

Most importantly it meant that David junior would not be forced to act according to his conscience, and 'grass' on the dealer. Nor would he have to face the wrath of his accomplices in or outside the courthouse, and Jonathan would hopefully not be placed in any awkward position.

There was a second, much less significant but altogether more immediate, consequence of the good news that had just heard.

Helen summarised it when she said, "Now we don't have to be home so early since we don't have to set off for Stonehaven in the morning."

She then followed up that declaration with an idea as to how to use the extra leisure time their phone call had afforded them. "How about ringing the Macleods to see if they are at home? We could go round and spend an hour or so with them if they are," she suggested.

When Rev. Donald Macleod had been forced to retire from his post as minister of the Church of Scotland owing to ill health, the family had left their home in the wild and lonely beauty of Kensalyre and resettled in Inverness. After some searching to find the number, a call to their friends of many years brought a very welcoming response.

"It's great to hear from you!" Peggy exclaimed. "And you are in Inverness! Come on round right away! We will be delighted to see you!"

It was a really happy reunion.

Aileen was on holiday from her job in Aberdeen, Mairi still hadn't returned to her studies in Edinburgh University after Easter, and David, who was married and living in Inverness, came around to join the party later. So David and Jonathan Runcie were reunited with all three of the Macleods with whom they had laughed and played for hours on end, roaming around in the wide-open spaces of Skye.

The parents had plenty to talk about, and so had their families. It was different, though, thirteen years on. The Macleod family, the carefree children of Skye, were now conscientious adults, and committed Christians. Two of them were married and working and the other was a university student.

The Runcie boys had arrived at that spur of the moment reunion on a different track entirely. One of them was a reformed drug addict who had forfeited a promising future because of his addiction and was trying, with the help of God, to fit all the shattered pieces together again. He had rededicated his life to the Lord and could enter into conversations on Christian topics with a knowledge born from experience.

The other lad, though, felt in a sense isolated. He was the only person there not a Christian, and although he was conscious of this, it didn't seem to make a bit of difference to anyone else. Conversely, he felt a wonderful awareness of acceptance, enveloped in the warm glow of genuine Christian care.

The question, "And what are you doing with yourself now?" brought a variety of interesting answers from the young men and women, all in their early-mid twenties, as they shared together. None, though, had as colourful a tale to tell as Jonathan. From fish factory to Art College, from sinking trawler to helicopter rescue, from into the harbour until out of the hospital, it had all been dramatic stuff. His had been a tempestuous, roller coaster, high-risk life. And he was still only twenty!

It was the kind of warm situation in which personal expression comes easily. So when Jonathan told his sympathetic audience that he had decided to try and get himself 'sorted out,' and had applied to Teen Challenge, they were immediately and enthusiastically supportive.

"I would like you to pray for me," Jonathan requested. It was an unusual entreaty, coming from the not yet entirely convinced young man, but the atmosphere made it easy, almost obligatory.

Then turning to look across at Mairi, his childhood friend, he said, "Maybe some of you will even come to see me if I go there."

When this observation failed to elicit any instant response, owing possibly to the practicalities involved, he amended his proposal to a more reasonable demand.

"Well, if you couldn't get to see me, which I suppose wouldn't be possible, you could at least write to me," he suggested. "I'm sure that would be a great help to me, and I would promise to write back."

Mairi recognised that these ostensibly general remarks were probably targeted at her, so she acted as spokesperson for everyone when she replied, "Let us know when you go down to Yorkshire, Jonathan, and we will all pray for you."

There was a brief pause, and then a smile creased her lips as she went on to volunteer, "And I will write to you. I promise."

Jonathan felt good during the long drive home. He hadn't really wanted to make the trip to Inverness that day, but recognised that he'd better go, for his own safety.

And it had all turned out so worthwhile, so unexpectedly.

It had been good to meet Mairi particularly again, and her promise to write to him would be a big bonus.

Would it help him to look upon Teen Challenge with any more than an offhand interest, though?

Or would he still consider himself conned by all these caring Christians?

Chapter 27
# I'M LAUGHING AT THE DEVIL!

In mid April news came through from Keighley.

Jonathan had been accepted for the Teen Challenge course commencing on Thursday 2nd May. As his mum and dad wished to visit Matthew, who was completing his course at the Teen Challenge Centre, Duns, in the Scottish Borders, they planned to leave a day early. On the evening of Tuesday April 30 th, before his planned departure for detox, quite a number of Jonathan's relatives came around to say their goodbyes to him and wish him every blessing. All their assurances that they were 'so glad for him,' that he was 'doing the right thing,' and that 'this was an answer to prayer,' didn't fire him up in the same way as it seemed to do for them.

They sounded thrilled at the thought of him setting off for Teen Challenge.

He felt tricked and revolted at the thought of it. What had he let himself in for?

Granny Runcie was one of the last to leave, but while she was still in, talking to his parents about meetings, Jonathan saw an opportunity to make a brief bid for freedom. He popped his head around the door where they were all engrossed in conversation to say, "I'm just nipping down to the garage to buy some sweets."

He was back in fifteen minutes with his 'sweets', which he didn't offer to 'share with everybody' as he had been taught to do as a boy. It is doubtful if they would have done his granny any good anyway!

When the last visitor had gone, Helen went to bed just before midnight. A few minutes later Jonathan shouted in to her that he to was 'off to bed.' He had possibly popped a few pills, but sounded in a good mood. Helen called, "Goodnight," to him, and then lay back to think how good it would be that by tomorrow night all three boys would be in rehab.

What an answer to prayer! Whether Jonathan liked it or not.

David came to bed around twelve-thirty and silence descended on the Runcie household. But not for long. Jonathan was to attempt an even more dramatic bid for freedom.

Helen's parent's car was parked in the driveway. Since her mum and dad were elderly and had been ill, their daughter had the use of the car to meet all their transport needs when required. The car keys hung on a hook in the kitchen amongst all the other household keys.

At twenty past one, the telephone rang.

David, who had just settled into a sound sleep, wondered, Who on earth is ringing at this time of night? It's likely those stupid taxis again! He reached out and picked up the receiver of the bedside telephone.

"Hello, is that Mr Runcie?" a man's voice enquired.

"Aye, it is," David grunted, sleepily.

"This is Fraserburgh Police Station," the caller went on. "Are you the owner of a blue Ford Fiesta, registration number L346 LSA?"

David had stirred himself awake at the sound of the familiar word 'police.' "No, we don't own it, but we are using it at the moment. It belongs to my in-laws," he volunteered.

"Do you know where the vehicle is at present, sir?" the friendly bobby went on to ask.

"Aye, I do," David told him, surprised at being asked such a ridiculous question. "It's parked in our driveway."

The policeman wondered if he wouldn't mind nipping out to check.

Rising reluctantly from his bed, David certainly wasn't going outside to look.

He pulled the curtains apart to take a peek.

The drive was empty. The car wasn't there!

When he returned to the phone, David had a confession to make. He had been wrong. The car wasn't where he thought it was. But where was it?

Fraserburgh Police had the answer to that. "You may be surprised to know," the policeman's voice drawled on, "Your car is embedded in the bushes on the by-pass. And your son Jonathan is in our cells. Would you care to come down to the station and make a statement?"

With all the commotion around her, Helen realised that something strange was going on. She could barely wait for her husband to replace the receiver before enquiring anxiously, "What's happening, David?"

"It sounds like a bad dream," David told her, pulling on his trousers. "Jonathan must have taken your mum and dad's car and has crashed it on the by-pass. Come on. We have to go down to the Police Station."

On arriving there, the policeman told Jonathan's parents a crazy story. They had apparently been alerted by some residents who had reported a car stuck amongst the bushes in a council flowerbed. Its engine was revving, its wheels spinning and its headlights blazing. When Jonathan saw the blue lights of the police car approaching he tried to make yet another bid for freedom. His legs refused to co-operate, though, and his brain wasn't working, owing to the 'sweets' he had been sucking. Unfortunately for him, neither was he any match for the strong arm of the law. The officers at the scene had handcuffed him despite him protesting that they were violating his human rights.

Jonathan was now detained in the cells.

After having made a joint statement, David and Helen were informed that their son was to be charged with multiple offences. The list was awesome. Stealing a car, driving without a licence, driving without insurance, driving under the influence of drugs and having his mother's bankcard in his possession.

His parents asked that these charges be dropped, as he was due to set off for a drugs rehabilitation centre in the morning. The interviewing officer pointed out the difficulty in that situation. "I'm sorry," he explained, "if these charges are dropped, you will be charged with collusion, in that you provided your son with the car in which he committed the other offences."

David had become exasperated by this time. "Well, if that's the case," he replied, rising from his seat, "let the law take its course. We have more immediate matters to attend to. There's a car to be pulled out of the bushes up on the by-pass."

On leaving the Police Station, David and Helen went straight to the council flowerbed to work out how to solve the problem. It was just after two o'clock in the morning, a thick Scottish drizzle threatened to soak them through, and the car was stuck fast. Any further revving of the engine would have the neighbours phoning the police a second time.

They needed two basic pieces of equipment. These were a saw with which to cut the surrounding bushes and a rope to tow the car off. They returned to the house for these items and set to work. It was a difficult, tiring, frustrating job. Eventually, though, after a number of fruitless attempts, with Helen at the wheel of her mum and dad's car, in that most unusual position, in the middle of the night, David was able to tow the car free.

Their problems weren't over even then, though. As they began to make their way home on the public road, Helen, realising that something was radically wrong with the car, flashed her lights to attract the attention of her husband who was driving ahead.

When they both stopped and examined the car, they discovered that Helen was driving on a flat front wheel. Their next job was to find the jack and change it!

It was half-past three in the morning when they arrived back into the house. They were both soaking wet. David's hands were cold and numb, cut and bleeding from his encounter with the bushes and covered with oil and grease from changing the wheel. Having washed his hands thoroughly in warm water to restore the circulation and remove the mess, he decided to make a cup of tea.

Helen who had gone to change out of her damp clothes, returned to the kitchen to find him convulsed with laughter. She found this most peculiar after all they had just been through.

"What do you think's so funny?" she enquired bewildered. She was concerned that perhaps Jonathan's attempts at rally driving had driven him round the bend.

When he regained sufficient composure to speak without laughing, David exclaimed with almost childish glee, "I'm just laughing at the devil!"

His wife looked at him strangely. "What do you mean, you're just laughing at the devil?" she enquired.

"He thought he could stop Jonathan going to rehab, but he's not going to win this one. God has proved once again that He is much stronger than the devil," David stated with a note of triumph.

The exhausted couple had barely been in bed for three hours when the phone rang again. Who else could it be but their friends at the Fraserburgh Police Station?

Could they come down and collect their son whom they were releasing from custody?

Yes, they could.

And they would shortly be taking him down the road to Keighley.

Chapter 28
# PRAISE GOD FOR MAIRI AND ROTTEN TEETH!

It had happened!

Jonathan had gone!

The house had become suddenly silent. There was now no TV in the middle of the night…no smell of smoke…no hash pipes…no clumping of feet on the stairs…no blaring music…no tinfoil below the bed…no tooters in the pillowslips…no weird characters at the door…and no need to tell visitors to look out for their wallets and purses.

Peace at last.

It was so amazing that Helen often had to pinch herself to make sure that she hadn't been transported on a magic carpet to Fantasyland. All three boys were now at different stages in the Teen Challenge programme.

To add to the increasing spiritual thrill, to which the once vexed parents were slowly becoming slowly acclimatised, young David asked his dad if he could be baptized the next time he came home for a weekend. This was gladly arranged, and on Sunday 7 th July 2002, David the dad baptized David the lad by immersion in Bethesda Evangelical Church. This baptism was a tremendous encouragement to the members of the fellowship, who had prayed faithfully for the family through all the ups and downs of the previous years. It was also to prove a particular delight to Helen's dad whose mobility was restricted, but who had made an enormous effort to attend the baptismal service.

Jonathan coped reasonably well with his induction month at the detox centre in Keighley. When he was transferred to South Wales to begin Phase 1 of the programme, though, he became unsettled and homesick.

The rules of the organisation hadn't allowed him any telephone contact with the outside world during his month in Keighley, but his first call home from South Wales was a cry for help.

"Mum, I need to ask you a question," he began. "I hate it here. I'm not doing good. If I leave and come home will you take me in?"

The tension seemed to travel up the line from Carmarthenshire to Aberdeenshire. Helen had to make a firm and fast decision.

"Sorry, Jonathan, you know that we told you before you left we wouldn't be taking you in again until you have completed the course."

"In that case, I'll have to make other plans," was the disgruntled student's disgruntled response. Jonathan sounded dejected. Would he stay the course or was he going to be the first one to opt out?

This was the first downer his mum had experienced for weeks. Reports from staff members had indicated that Jonathan was settling in well and making satisfactory progress. The picture he had painted was entirely different. It was especially designed to play on his mother's emotions.

In the weeks that were to follow, Jonathan adapted his report to suit the parent he was speaking to. It was invariably, 'I'm doing fine', to dad, and 'doom and gloom' to mum. On gaining her ear, on one particular occasion he confessed, "You know, I wouldn't be staying in this place at all if it weren't for two things. Firstly, I'm getting free dental treatment for my rotten teeth, and the other thing is that Mairi is writing to me regularly and she tells me she is praying for me too."

After that telephone conversation, Helen caught her husband passing through the hall and remarked with an amused expression, "Praise God for Mairi and rotten teeth!"

The continued contact with Wales began to indicate a mellowing in Jonathan's approach. Could his mum and dad dare to hope that his hard heart was softening?

At the beginning, he had remarked sarcastically to his mum, "They are all just full of it here." 'It' being presumably the Christian Gospel.

In a subsequent letter, however, he divulged, "I'm trying not to fight it." 'It' was obviously making an impression.

Just as David and Helen were allowing themselves to tentatively imagine that God was beginning to work in the life of their rebellious, headstrong son, he suffered a demoralising setback

Another student had been taunting Jonathan mercilessly when the hot temper, which had been the bane of his life since boyhood, flared up. In a moment of madness he made a swipe at his tormentor. And the most galling aspect of the whole incident for Jonathan was that he chose to do it in full view of one of the staff members, who had no choice but to intervene and then report the incident.

Violence of any sort is not tolerated in Teen Challenge and could, in extreme cases, lead to the perpetrator being sent home. When the management came to consider Jonathan's case they recognised that there were mitigating circumstances. For one thing he had been an exemplary student up until that moment, and was making excellent progress in the programme. The staff member who had reported Jonathan's rush of blood to the head had also testified that he was being 'mercilessly provoked.'

Having considered all the evidence, and well aware that

a sending home could easily lead to a return to drugs, the Teen Challenge management decided to punish Jonathan by returning him to Keighley to commence the course all over again.

This was a hard blow to take, a bitter pill to swallow. He was going to be put back twelve weeks. All he wanted to do now was pack it all in and head for home. He didn't though. Mairi was only one of many who were praying earnestly, daily, for him. And the staff members kept encouraging him to see it through.

It was then that God intervened.

In mid-September Jonathan's mum and dad received an unexpected letter in which he began by recounting how he had 'just happened' to be reading, out of boredom rather than interest, the eighteenth Psalm. Suddenly verses 16-19 jumped up out of the page at him.

*'He sent from on high; He took me; He drew me out of many waters.*

*He delivered me from my strong enemy, and from those who hated me: for they were too mighty for me.*

*They confronted me in the day of my calamity: but the Lord was my stay.*

*He brought me forth into a broad place; He rescued me, because He delighted in me.'*

is what he read.

Jonathan described in his letter how he felt on discovering these words of the psalmist. The free expression of his full heart was such a tonic to the soul that Helen read the letter over about twenty times before ever putting it down. She was overcome by unsurpassed spiritual delight and unbounded gratitude to God.

'…Listen,' he wrote. *'He sent from on high; He took me; He drew me out of many waters.'*

Now, I've always looked back on my life and thought, 'Wow, I've had a lot of near misses! I've been pretty lucky.' It never occurred to me that maybe God had something to do with it! Obviously, you both know about my close shaves with the water! The first time I fell in the harbour. The second was when the boat sank (we were saved just in time!) And the third was the overdose. It says 'He drew me out of many waters,' and now I realize He did. Literally!

Verse 17 goes on to say, *'He delivered me from my strong enemy, and from those who hated me, for they were too mighty for me.'*

Well, when I came to T.C. I didn't think at first I'd been 'delivered' by God, but there was one thing I knew for sure. Drugs were a 'strong enemy' for me! And very quickly I found that they were also 'too mighty for me.'

When someone has an enemy, something always happens. There is a fight. A battle. I tried different methods to stop the effect drugs (especially heroin) were having on my life. Do you remember the prescriptions? Even though that didn't work, I had hoped it would. I even tried taking money out of the equation by stopping the sea. As you know, that didn't work either. Drugs were simply too strong for me.

Verse 18 says, *'They confronted me in the day of my calamity, but the Lord was my stay.'*

Now I realize that, as my problems were coming to a point where I couldn't handle them any more, God was in control. 'The Lord was my stay.'

I used to reason and say to myself, 'Did God bring me here?'

For a long time my answer was No. I just ended up here because of what was happening in my life, a few months before. I thought, 'God didn't bring me here. It was the problems in my life.'

At the end of the day it doesn't matter **how** He got me here. His thinking is beyond ours. *'For my thoughts are not your thoughts, nor are your ways my ways, declares the Lord.' (Isaiah 55 v. 8 )* So now I know it was Him who brought me here.

Verse 19 reads, *'He brought me into a broad place; He rescued me because he delighted in me.'*

For me, the broad place is T.C. obviously. But sometimes I do ask, 'Why me? Why, God, did you bother rescuing me?' The answer is simply because 'He delighted in me.' That's why it's so hard to walk away from this now. Because God has promised something better.

Whenever I feel like giving this up and walking away I have another good verse I think about. Listen, *'For consider your calling, brethren, that there were not many wise according to the flesh, not many mighty, not many noble,'* and, *'But God has chosen the* **FOOLISH** *things of the world to confound the wise…'*

I think I qualify for that! Don't you? Ha! Ha!

Well, better go. Thank you for the Bible. I'm very happy with it. Tell granny and granda J. and granny Runcie thank you as well.

Take care. God bless,
Jonno.'

The next time Jonathan rang home his mum and dad told him of the tremendous pleasure his letter had brought them. They couldn't find words to express their joy. It was wonderful. Unbelievable! Helen was now to back pinching herself every ten or fifteen minutes!

Jonathan had obviously become aware of the preserving hand of God in his life, and within weeks he was to experience the power of God to provide for him also.

By that time a third element had been added to free dental treatment and Mairi's letters and prayers as a reason to keep Jonathan persisting with the programme. It was his passionate desire to learn to play the guitar.

He had picked up a guitar in the chapel at Keighley one day and had begun to strum on it for something to do. There were a number of 'communal' instruments in the building and the lads were encouraged to play them in their spare time. With his musical background Jonathan realized that playing the guitar came almost as second nature to him. In three or four days time he was spending every free minute he had in the chapel, practising, practising, practising.

His desire to become proficient on the instrument helped him settle again during his 'repeat', punishment month, but as it came near an end, Jonathan remembered something that was a shock to the musical system.

There were no communal guitars in South Wales! All the guys who played musical instruments of any sort down there owned them! What was he going to do? He was due to return to Phase 1 for a second time in less than a fortnight, but he viewed the prospect of life without a guitar in the same way as he had viewed the overall prospect of Teen Challenge at the start. It would be abject misery.

Lying in bed one night a voice seemed to say to him, 'Talk to God about it.'

He ignored it.

Next night there came this same thought. 'You should pray to God for a guitar.'

It sounded crazy. How could God provide him with a guitar? He wasn't allowed to go out to shops, and anyhow, even if he were, he didn't have any money. And guitars were costly items.

When the suggestion that he should pray for a guitar just refused to go away, Jonathan prayed a most unusual prayer one night. "God," he began, "something has been telling me to ask You for a guitar. I don't know how You are going to do this, but could You bring somebody with a guitar to sell across my path? And please God I need it before the end of next week, and the most I can afford is twenty pounds. Thank You, God. Amen."

Having made his first 'guitar prayer' to God, the urge to repeat it became increasingly strong and so every morning and night Jonathan asked God for a guitar. His natural common sense, however, told him that it was impossible. God didn't just drop guitars from the skies on to people's heads. What Jonathan forgot was that He had His servants on earth.

One evening, four days before he was due to return to South Wales, Jonathan was standing in the lobby of the centre. A staff member whom he had only previously seen at a distance came across to speak to him.

"I know we haven't been much in contact," he began, almost apologetically, "but I have been waiting for an opportunity to see you alone for some time. I have something for you. It is out in the car. If you wait there a minute I will go out and bring it in."

When the staff member came back a few minutes later he was carrying a guitar case. Jonathan's eyes almost popped out of his head.

He stood the case on the floor and then, half leaning on it, went on to explain, "I have just had the most peculiar experience. I have three guitars and the Lord has been telling me for the last day or two to give you one of them."

Jonathan was awestruck.

And there was more.

The staff member paused, swallowed hard, and then went

on, "I was going to give you the cheapest one but God said No, you must give him your best. I gave my Son, the best thing I had for you, so I want you to give him your best for Me.' So here it is, my best guitar."

He then took a step forward and reached the dumbfounded Jonathan the case, which he unzipped to reveal a most beautiful 'Washburn' guitar. Jonathan was absolutely astounded. He had wanted to buy a guitar from somebody for twenty pounds at the most. Here was a man giving him a guitar worth hundreds.

As the overwhelmed recipient began to stutter his thanks, the staff member said, "Don't thank me, Jonathan. Thank God." And with that he turned and left the lobby, closing the door gently behind him.

When Jonathan had returned to his bedroom and given his gift from God a thorough examination he began to play it. The tone was fantastic. It was a marvellous instrument, the best he had ever seen, or heard, in his guitar experience.

Jonathan was soon on his knees again. "Thank You, God for answering my prayers," he said simply. He found it difficult to articulate his deep appreciation, but had no difficulty in expressing an awakening desire. "I want to do business with You," he concluded.

When people show a genuine interest in 'doing business with' God, He always takes the lead in the negotiations. That's what Jonathan was to find out after returning to Wales.

As he began to read his Bible more avidly, and listen to the programme leaders more intently, he discovered that although he had come to appreciate something of the infinite power of God, he knew little of the Lord Jesus. And he wanted to remedy that.

Reading the Gospels prayerfully he realised that it was true what God had told the staff member who had given him his guitar. God had given His only Son to come into the world to die on a cross to take away his sins. And that it was possible to have a personal, vital relationship with Him. All he had to do was accept Jesus as his Saviour and Lord.

One evening, alone in his room, Jonathan did just that. "Lord Jesus, I want to know Your presence in my life. Come in and reveal Yourself to me, and help me to live for You every day," he prayed.

It was simple, but it was all that was required.

The God who had been his Divine Deliverer and his Practical Provider had now become his Personal Saviour.

Praise God for new life in Christ!

Praise God for His obedient servant and his sacrificial gift of a cherished guitar!

And praise God for Mairi and rotten teeth!

Chapter 29
# WHAT REJOICING!

It was so frustrating.

David and Helen were stuck in a horrendous traffic jam on the way to the ferry port of Ijmuiden near Amsterdam at the end of their summer holiday in early August 2002. Helen had been upset to learn that her mum and dad were both ill and in hospital at home. All she wanted to do was to get there to be with them.

This anxiety led to an increasing sense of panic that they were going to miss the ferry. A rock music festival was taking place a few miles up the road, and four lanes of traffic had come to a complete standstill in the blistering heat.

Unknown to them, the departure time of the ferry had been put back as most of its prospective passengers had been caught up in the gridlock like themselves. This meant that David and Helen need not have been so keyed up and they made it on time.

When they did eventually arrive home, Helen's first stop was the hospital to visit her parents. Both were seriously ill, and the prognosis wasn't good for either. At one stage, the hospital staff thought that her mum was in more danger than her dad, but when it became established that her dad would be unable to undergo essential surgery, the picture changed.

Those were distressing days. As David and Helen travelled to the hospital in Aberdeen to visit the elderly couple in separate wards, they were touched by their interest in the family. Despite their illness, they never lost their concern for the boys and their well-being.

Mum and dad Johnston had lived and prayed through the darkest of days with the family, and were now so encouraged that the boys were now all at Teen Challenge.

Perhaps it was a throwback to the morning when Jonathan had lost his temper, and granda Johnston had sat leaning on his stick muttering, 'O Jonathan, O Jonathan,' that he would ask occasionally with genuine care, "How's Jonathan doing?"

In late September, Helen's mum was well enough to be discharged from hospital, but not well enough to go home to live by herself, so she came to stay with her daughter and son-in-law. It was by then an ideal convalescent home, for there were no boys around to increase the tension levels. There would be no TV in the middle of the night, no banged doors, and no yelled objections!

For dad, though, things were different. He had been out at David's baptism in July, and although he wasn't aware of it at the time, that church service, which had afforded him such joy and pleasure, was to be the last he would attend.

His condition began to deteriorate, slowly at first, then more rapidly.

It soon became obvious that he wouldn't be coming home. He passed away to be with the Lord, whom he had loved and served for so many years, on October 9 th.

The prospect of a funeral meant that the three grandsons had to be transported from all 'arts and parts' to attend. David was in Carlisle working for Youth With A Mission. This was accepted by Teen Challenge as phase 4 of his programme. Matthew, who had begun first, and was farthest through the programme, was within days of his graduation, and Jonathan was still on his 'return trip' to Keighley.

In spite of the distances involved, and the problems

associated with travel arrangements, the boys co-operated with their parents to ensure that they all arrived home in good time.

What a contrast to the family gathering at David's dad's funeral three years before. This was the first time that the three boys had been together since Matthew had gone away to rehab, and it was, despite the reason for the get-together, a glad reunion. Although Helen was grieving for her dad, she was so happy to have her three sons together again under the same roof, and all 'clothed and in their right minds.' They too were pleased to be with one another, and used the occasion to spend time, sharing their experiences of Teen Challenge, and laughing at some of the incidents in which they had been involved in days gone by.

Their mum noticed the biggest difference on the day of the funeral itself. She didn't have to chase them around the house that morning with a tie in one hand, and a pair of shoes in the other, calling out, 'Here put these on,' or, 'is this one yours?'

Each lad was able to sort out what he himself wanted to wear. It seemed so basic, but for the Runcie household, it was a massive advance, brought about only by the power of God.

When the family were discussing the seating arrangements for the funeral, and because David was playing the organ, Helen had two simple requests to make. The first was that as the only daughter, she would like to sit with her mum. Her other was that as a thankful mother she insisted on having her rehabilitated family around her.

The weather was bright and sunny and Helen set out for the church with a rare amalgam of emotion. She was sorry to have lost her dad but glad to have regained her sons. Her dad had gone to heaven to be with Christ, and her three happy, healthy looking, well-dressed sons had created for her a foretaste of heaven on earth.

As the service progressed she became conscious of a dual responsibility. Her deeply grieving mother was on one side of her and her three 'returned prodigals' on the other.

It was a sad, glad, grief-stricken, joyful event.

The service ended with the singing of a well-known hymn. It was one which Helen had heard sung at possibly hundreds of funerals before, and that day she sang with mixed emotions all the way through it.

The chorus described the position of privilege to which her dad had been promoted upon his passing.

'Face to face shall I behold Him,
Far beyond the starry sky;
Face to face in all His glory,
I shall see Him by and by!'

everyone sang heartily. It was peculiar. Helen felt almost obliged to be weeping but if her dad had realised that ultimate goal of the Christian, and had seen the face of Jesus, why should she weep for him? During the service the congregation had been reminded that James Johnston was now 'with Christ, which is far better.' If that were so, and her dad had been transported to that realm of bliss from a debilitating illness in a hospital bed why should she, or any of the other Christian members of the family for that matter, be mourning as though there were no hope or joy up ahead?

When they came to the third verse of the hymn Helen was so overcome with what the Bible describes as 'beauty for ashes, and the oil of joy for mourning,' that she had to stop singing altogether.

She merely turned her head to her left to look and listen. And what she saw and heard filled her with an unbelievable sense of gratitude to God. The strong voices of her three adult sons boomed out beside her in words that made her feel almost like collapsing to her knees to cry out in awesome wonder.

'What rejoicing in His presence,
When are banished grief and pain;
When the crooked ways are straightened,
And the dark things shall be plain,'

was what they were singing so lustily.

The words struck a tender chord in Helen's heart.

There had been a lot of 'crooked ways straightened' already for the once often mystified Runcies, and many dark, apparently inexplicable things, already made 'plain.'

'What rejoicing in His presence.'

That would be for the future.

What rejoicing in His power.

That was certainly for the present.

What rejoicing!

What rejoicing!

What rejoicing!

Would there be, could there be, any end to it?

Chapter 30
# NOW WE ARE A FAMILY AGAIN!

The family had come together again in love, in the Lord, and in love for the Lord.

It was marvellous, and it was a story worth telling.

In the early months of 2003 when David and Helen were invited to speak or sing at Church engagements they began to bring at least one of the boys along, depending on who happened to be free and at home at the time. God had done so much in all five lives that they were always both willing and eager to tell others about it to give Him the glory.

Mark 'Tatty' Gordon, a converted addict and now community drugs counsellor in Bangor, Northern Ireland, invited David to address a weekend seminar on the drugs issue in the Shiloh Fellowship in the County Down town in April 2003. The aim of the Saturday workshop was to examine the part local churches could play in tackling the increasing drugs problem in the district.

David Runcie was ideally equipped to share in such a venture. As a founder member of the Fraserburgh Drugs Awareness Strategy Group, and with his involvement in the very worthwhile Solid Rock Café, he had a wealth of organisational experience in the field. Such background knowledge would no doubt be useful, but the title of the seminar, 'It's Different When It's Your Own,' summed up his most valuable qualification succinctly. When addressing the conference David wasn't merely quoting statistics or proposing strategies. He was speaking from practical personal experience, and that made all the difference.

One of the most appreciated elements of the Saturday morning session was that both David the younger and Jonathan had joined their dad for the weekend in Northern Ireland. They were available to chat to everyone during the coffee breaks and share their stories. Their presence had the potential to make more of an impact than David's entire discourse.

Their dad recognised this and remarked at the end of his presentation, "The fact that two of my sons are here with me today is proof that God is still running His rescue shop. These lads have found new life in Christ and are building a new life for themselves in His service after drugs."

When the seminar was over David and the two boys took a walk down into Bangor town centre. As they sat having a meal in an Indian restaurant the dad noticed that Jonathan looked decidedly uncomfortable. And it was no wonder. His son had survived the latter half of his teenage years on a diet of hard drugs, sweet snacks and sugary drinks, and was still on the Teen Challenge programme. He couldn't remember the last time he had ever been in a restaurant. It was all so strange, so formal.

Life after drugs, even life in the Lord after drugs, was to prove a long, slow, learning curve.

On the next day, Sunday 6 th April, David had been invited to speak in two different churches. In the morning he was responsible for the service in Shiloh Christian Fellowship in Bangor and then he took the evening service at the Independent Methodist Church, in Coleraine, County Londonderry.

Rev. Eric Stewart asked David and Jonathan to tell bits of their life stories in the service in Coleraine and this caused quite a stir amongst the congregation. Few, if any of them had ever heard two brothers, who had been through so much together when drug addicts in earlier life, speak. They were moved to see them standing up to recount something of God's amazing grace in their lives.

The warmth of the welcome they were accorded by everyone in the course of the weekend made David and Jonathan feel both thankful and humble all at once. They were thankful to God to have been rescued from a life of sin but humble that it should have been necessary in the first place. And that it should have been them. Many of their mates from days gone past had died of overdoses.

A number expressed genuine interest in them as young Christians with a vision of seeing others in similar circumstances led to coming off drugs and coming to Christ. They promised, with undoubted conviction, to pray for God's guidance in their lives.

Jonathan fell in love with Northern Ireland and the uncomplicated sincerity of its Christian people over that April weekend, and decided to return there to complete Phase 4, the practical part of his Teen Challenge programme, if possible.

Just over a week later, back in Scotland, it was Matthew's turn to share the story of what God had done in his life with an appreciative congregation. His mum had been asked to address the Ladies Fellowship of the Burghead Free Church of Scotland. In the course of the service she related some of the amazing ways in which God had answered prayer for her family and David and she sang a few pieces.

Then Matthew spoke.

He told something of his background and of the sense of joy and freedom he now felt having been liberated from the iron grip of drugs. His most telling contribution, though, was when he reached for his guitar and began to sing the worship song, 'How Deep The Father's Love For Us.'

Every word seemed to explode with meaning and feeling as he sang,

> 'How deep the Father's love for us,
> How vast beyond all measure,
> That He should give His only Son,
> To make a wretch His treasure…'

The change in Matthew's life, and his recognition of the wonder of it all was evident when he came to the final verse when he sang with a air of devotion and dedication,

> 'I will not boast in anything,
> No gifts, no power, no wisdom,
> But I will boast in Jesus Christ,
> His death and resurrection.
> Why should I gain from His reward?
> I cannot give an answer,
> But this I know with all my heart,
> His wounds have paid my ransom.'

The atmosphere had suddenly become charged with an almost tangible reverence. God, through Matthew, had created a climate of spiritual expectancy. David had no difficulty in bringing a closing thought about His love and power and grace after that. Matthew had been the same to his parents in Scotland as the other two sons had been to their dad back in Northern Ireland. They were walking, talking, praying, praising visual aids.

The Runcie family reached hitherto unattainable heights of spiritual joy and delight on Saturday 17 th May, 2003. At the end of April Matthew and Jonathan had expressed a desire to be baptised, and the baptismal service was arranged for that evening.

Every available seat in Bethesda Evangelical Church was taken, well before the service was due to begin. The place was packed. Hundreds of people had been praying for 'the Runcie boys' down the years, and any of those who were within travelling distance, and were free on that particular date, made a point of being there. They were anxious to see God's response to their requests worked out to a heart-warming climax before their very eyes.

Nor were they disappointed.

David led the meeting and the first family member to take part in the service was his oldest son, David junior. He read a most relevant Scripture portion for such a gathering. Like his brothers, David could empathise in many respects with the main character depicted in the reading from Luke chapter 15 vs. 11 – 24, the prodigal son. All three of them were well acquainted with distance from God, and the degradation of sin, from their encounters with drugs. They were there that evening, however, to rejoice in the delight of their Heavenly Father at their return. That reading set the scene and the theme for the evening.

Next up were David and Helen singing together a hymn that had become most precious to them through the darkest of days in the previous three or four years.

When Helen sang the first verse as a solo piece every vestige of her being was in it and behind it. She identified with every word, and so did many in the congregation, for they had joined in the 'tears and sorrows' with her. An intense silence, a holy hush, hung over the church as she sang,

'I've had many tears and sorrows, I've had questions for tomorrow,
There have been times I didn't know right from wrong.
But in every situation, God gave blessed consolation,
That my trials come to only make me strong...'

David then joined in with the chorus and the pair sang together with voices in harmony and lives ripened to maturity with the searing heat of successive testing,

'Through it all, through it all,
I have learned to trust in Jesus,
I have learned to trust in God.
Through it all, through it all,
I have learned to depend upon His Word.'

Matthew and Jonathan then told the congregation of how they had come to know the Lord, and what He meant to them. The easy, natural, unaffected nature of their approach and the obvious depth of their new relationship with God were most compelling.

'I wake up in the morning and I'm absolutely buzzing. I can't wait to get out of bed. I've got a real zeal just now," Jonathan testified enthusiastically, just in case somebody hadn't noticed. "I just want to get into that water and dedicate my life to God. And when I say He is my Lord, I mean He is my Lord. I love You Jesus. Amen."

When Matthew rose to speak he said that the early verses of Ephesians chapter two in the Bible summarised his life, both before and after conversion. He confessed that every time he read them they 'hit home.' When he proceeded to read the verses in question, everybody understood what he meant.

'...In time past you walked according to the course of this world, according to the prince of the power of the air, the spirit that is now at work in the children of disobedience...

But God, who is rich in mercy, for his great love wherewith he loved us,

Even when we were dead in sins, has made us alive together

*with Christ, (by grace you are saved;)*

*And has raised us up together, and made us sit together in heavenly places in Christ Jesus:*

*That in the ages to come he might show the exceeding riches of his grace in his kindness toward us through Christ Jesus.*

*For by grace are you saved through faith; and that not of yourselves: it is the gift of God:*

*Not of works, lest any man should boast...'*

As Matthew was making his way down from the platform, his dad stopped him.

He then beckoned to Helen and the other two boys to join them at the front of the church. After a moment's hesitation Jonathan, David and Helen filed up. The boys wondered what was going on, for whatever it was, nobody had ever told them about it.

They needn't have worried. It was just one of their dad's spur of the moment decisions. He had an instant inspiration. The family had been praising the Lord for His goodness, individually. Now he saw a way that this could be done collectively.

When all five Runcies were lined up at the front, boys in the middle and mum and dad at either end, David had an announcement to make.

"I just want to say, to give Him the glory," he began, "this is what God does."

He looked along the line-up before going on, his voice on the verge of breaking, "He not only saves souls. He restores lives. These three were lost to us. They were dead. Now we are a family again! "

There was barely a dry eye in the building.

The hankies were out all over the audience. Again.

# 2012
# UPDATE

Chapter 31
# THROUGH IT ALL

The launch of the first edition of this book, 'Out of the Deep,' on 27 th November, 2003, in Fraserburgh Leisure Centre, proved a special landmark in the lives of David and Helen Runcie. They had become used to going there for a variety of Christian events, such as the Gospel Music Convention and prayer breakfasts.

This, though, was something completely different.

In one sense it was the end, the culmination, of a research project. They had made a number of trips across the Irish Sea to recount their story to the author, or alternatively entertained him in their home, for that same reason. This process had taken nine months. Now the fruit of their labours was about to go on public sale.

Yet they were not to realise fully at the time, how this night was also set to impact the remainder of their lives. Little did they know that Friday night would mark not only the launch of a book but also the initiation of a contact ministry that would be used to bring significant blessing to many hurting families. Though this book would be reckoned of little relevance in the eyes of the world, God had His plans to use it in reaching out to others who were, as they had once been, in seemingly helpless and hopeless situations.

Much planning had gone into the evening and David and Helen were eagerly anticipating, but also a little apprehensive about, the event. Doubts ran like wildfire through their minds.

'Would the people who were invited turn up?' they wondered.

"Are we really doing the right thing here?" they thought.

"Will the book sell?" they asked themselves.

Despite their anxieties, misgivings and emotional ups and downs they were excited and expectant. David and Helen believed this book had been in the plan and purpose of God, right from they had begun working on it. They had no option but to leave it to Him to work things out.

Having their family with them, along with their local church family, many friends and invited guests, made the evening special in itself. However, there was also an evident sense of the presence of God as various people shared in word and song. That book launch evening was everything David and Helen had hoped it would be.

The author shared his experiences in writing the book. Sam Gordon, a close family friend, recalled how he spent hours with the distraught parents throughout the drugs-devastated days, and the gradual, then total, transformation in the household when the boys one by one accepted Jesus into their lives.

Local singing group, 'New Life,' sang, 'Is Anything Too Hard for God?'One of the verses summed up David and Helen's experience precisely. It said,

'It's out of your hands, you've done all you can do;
You've given God the problem; it's no longer up to you.'

Annita McDonnell sang, 'The Anchor Holds.' Again the words ministered powerfully of God's ability to keep and sustain them through the storm they had weathered.

One of the most poignant moments came when David and Helen sang a song they had come to love. It was the one they had sung that memorable May night and were to sing again hundreds of times at church gatherings large and small over the next few years. Andrae Crouch's classic, 'Through it All,' had become their testimony song.

'Through it all, through it all,
I've learned to trust in Jesus,
I've learned to trust in God,
Through it all, through it all,
I've learned to depend upon His Word.

Those memorable moments in Fraserburgh were to be repeated the following evening in a church in Buckie, 50 miles along the Moray coast. A large number of books were purchased at both events. Some of these were bought by friends of the Runcie family, but many more by people they had never met before, and some by parents who had gone through, or were still languishing in the throes of, the same trauma as David and Helen had once experienced.

In the years that followed they had many opportunities to share in large gatherings, small groups or meet with hurting individuals in their own homes. During these encounters the couple shared in a simple and very personal way the highs and lows of the dark days, always acknowledging God's abiding presence and daily supplies of grace. Whether it was a formal Sunday service, a seminar, a women's meeting or a men's fellowship, they always concluded with their signature song, 'Through It All.'

Most of these meetings were in their native Scotland but David and Helen addressed, and sang at, gatherings in England and Ireland as well. There was also, in more recent years, a foreign aspect to their ministry when they were invited to speak at meetings in Kenya and Croatia, often with the help of an interpreter.

These experiences confirmed to David and Helen that wherever one goes in the world there are families torn apart by drug addiction or some form of substance misuse. There are many honourable organisations and government bodies trying hard to reduce the problem.

The parents from Fraserburgh can testify, though, that it is only God who can totally transform a life which is heading for destruction. Furthermore, it is only God who can sustain the parents or other family members through the pain and hurt of these dark days.

David and Helen have counselled and prayed with many people since this book was first published in November, 2003. Some of them they never heard from again, but a link was formed with others and lines of communication were established. A number of these contacts report thankfully how God answered prayer in their circumstances. Others are still waiting for the breakthrough.

It has been a privilege to witness how the book was used of God to bless so many distressed parents and despairing drug addicts during the past nine years. The family was amazed at the many copies sold and they remain astonished by the fact that people are even now still asking for it. Copies were placed in libraries, Teen Challenge and other drug rehab centres, drop-in centres and prisons. 'Out of the Deep' was also featured in newspapers and was favourably reviewed in Christian magazines.

The reaction from those who actually read the book was consistently most encouraging and is a subject in itself, calling for a chapter on its own.

Chapter 32
# WHAT A TESTIMONY!

David and Helen have felt privileged and somewhat humbled that God has been pleased to use the story of His presence in their trial to touch so many lives. They received many letters, emails and phone calls to either say thanks, share experiences or request help.

Extracts from a few of these letters/emails are given below but with names withheld in most cases to maintain confidentiality.

**Airdrie, Scotland.** "Thank you for allowing 'Out of the Deep' to be written. It is a great book and I am sure lots of parents will be able to relate to it. I have two sons, one of whom has never caused me any problems. However, my other son started to go off the rails from the age of 15, first with drink and then later with drugs... I went through all the things you both did until he asked for help... He eventually got a place at a Christian Rehabilitation Centre... Six months later he is still there. He has let the Lord into his heart and is doing wonderful and is baptised..."

**Glasgow, Scotland.** "We have a son who is 19 and has been smoking cannabis for quite a while... I feel I could understand totally some of the things you wrote... How you coped with three I don't know. .. Glasgow is a big city compared to Fraserburgh yet the problems are the same. How we need to pray for our young folk today. I have a cousin who is not a Christian but has heard about you. I will pass on my copy to her."

**Fraserburgh, Scotland.** "I bought your book yesterday at 4.40pm and finished it at 9 minutes past midnight. I just wanted you to know I am full of admiration for you all and what you have coped with. It is a truly excellent story. So harrowing at times and yet so full of hope..."

**Banff, Scotland.** "... I can't thank you all enough for allowing us into your home to speak openly about our son. Please pass on our thanks to Matthew, Ashley and Jonathan for the encouragement they offered concerning him..."

**Grimsby, England.** "I was preaching last Saturday at the Grimsby Bible Convention... During the tea break, a lady came up to me and said she had read through 'Out of the Deep' and then passed it on to her daughter who also read it through in one sitting. She said her daughter had plenty of time on her hands. As it turns out, her daughter is currently in a prison near Wakefield serving a sentence for drug dealing... It's amazing where that book is turning up!" Dr. Sam Gordon.

**Aberdeen, Scotland.** "... I am a Sunday School teacher and the admin assistant and web designer for my church and we will be starting a youth cell soon. At a recent meeting in our church, the senior pastor talked to us about getting someone in to talk about drug addiction. He wanted our members to be fully informed about this area and not be ignorant of it. After reading Noel Davidson's book I could not think of anyone better than your family to speak to us..."

**Brandenburg, Germany.** "Dear Helen, thank you so much for your book – what a testimony! I've told loads of people."

**Penzance, Cornwall, England.** "I have just finished reading 'Out of the Deep'... Having started the book I just couldn't put it down! ... I have passed on our copy to Christian friends in Devon who have a son with drug problems. What a wise and caring God we have! Praise Him!"

**Turiff, Aberdeenshire, Scotland.** "Thank you so much for seeing me last night. It was so kind of you to see me and listen to my story... Now we enter into the waiting period which I know will be hard all round... Please thank Jonathan and Matthew for talking to me, a complete stranger."

**Bristol, England.** "We have now both finished reading your book, 'Out of the Deep,' and just wanted to say how thrilled we are for you all. Your troubles and heartaches seemed never ending yet the Lord has brought you into a place of praise and rejoicing..."

**Glasgow, Scotland.** "Thank you so much for sending the books and signing them for us. What can I say? It is brilliantly written and so glorifying to God... It will be a great help to families who find themselves in the same circumstances, but what an encouragement to those who are wondering whether the Lord is still at work! ... I am writing to ask you to send me some more books as, when I have shared with people here about your story, the interest has been amazing."

**HM Prison, Peterhead, Scotland.** "I am writing because at 3.22 am this morning I read the final words of 'Out of the Deep.' The book was sent to me by a member of your church. I want to thank you all for your courage to share your anguish, suffering and torment. I want to thank you for the joy your book gave me... A fellow inmate is struggling with a drug problem and without Jesus will most certainly return to heroin on his release. The positive thing is that although he claims to be an atheist, he asked to read the book. Pray for him please... I cannot count the times I cried out for you all in your suffering, but not all of these tears together could match the tears of joy I shed as each time the light of love answered the prayers of parents, family and friends."

One of the most poignant and heart-warming letters David and Helen received came from someone they know very well, and who lives in the nearby town of Peterhead. It is included with just a minimum of editing.

"When I spoke to you recently you may have been surprised that I had not mentioned or purchased a copy of 'Out of the Deep.' In fact I had bought a copy in Peterhead and in my reading I'd reached the place where the choir (Fraserburgh Gospel Male Voice Choir) were leaving the Isle of Lewis.

Unlike some who could not put the book down without finishing it, I resolved to limit my reading to basically one chapter per evening, so that I could take time to digest every disappointment, challenge and comfort that you experienced.

You may find it hard to believe but I knew nothing of your sons' involvement in the drugs scene apart from one whisper shortly before you shared our pulpit with one of them, one Sunday morning... Although I am not usually a weepy person, I could not take in what I heard and cried for most of the service. In fact at one stage I felt I was going to have to leave the Kirk early...

Neither of you will ever know how deeply I felt for you both that day. I even found it emotionally difficult to relate to my wife what I had heard, on returning home.

Let me commend you for being so open and frank about your experiences as recorded in your book. The intense struggle experienced by a butterfly in the chrysalis stage creates veins strong enough to support flimsy wings which in turn bring beauty to our gardens in summer. Likewise you, by having laid bare your souls and without holding anything back, have enhanced the gospel of Christ and I believe 'Out of the Deep' will be used of God in several ways.

1- By encouraging parents of a wayward family member that there is hope for their son or daughter.

2 - By acting as a deterrent to young folk when they find themselves in a vulnerable position where they are tempted to 'try it for fun.'

3 - By showing young people who are heavily into drugs that there is a way back to God and good health.

4 - Finally, by demonstrating to others who are involved in the work of rescuing vulnerable teenagers that their efforts are not in vain.

I have enjoyed the occasions when I have heard David preach and I appreciate the times I've heard Helen sing... but I believe 'Out of the Deep' is by far the best message either of you ever preached or sang.

Thank you again for having the courage to make your story available to all and Mr. Davidson is to be complimented for making it so readable by young and old, and Christian and unbeliever alike..."

If David and Helen were to include all the correspondence they have received over the past nine years it would require, they tell us, a book on its own. There is, however, one individual in whose life the book was a key element in the hand of God as he experienced salvation and freedom from addiction...

Martin's story is coming next!

Chapter 33
# SICK AND TIRED OF BEING SICK AND TIRED

In his position as a social worker in a community support team specialising in the area of learning difficulties, David often had to meet with care providers from the private sector as well as voluntary agencies and other local government resources. The manager of one of these private agencies David used occasionally to provide care and support for his clients was aware that 'Out of the Deep' was due to be published in around six weeks. She knew why the book was being written and was familiar with the heartbreaking circumstances which had given rise to it.

Unknown to David this manager had an admin assistant who had confided in her about a problem which was causing her a great deal of distress and concern. The issue involved her brother who had a long standing problem with drug addiction. The situation was further compounded by the fact that she lived with her husband and family in northeast Aberdeenshire and her brother was still at home with their mother in Ayrshire, around 200 miles away.

This employee knew the situation at home was far from satisfactory and although she was concerned for her brother she was probably even more worried about her mother. Surely it must be extremely stressful having a son with a drug addiction problem living in the same house. In her desperation to find some help she had confided in her employer, the lady whom David had informed about the book launch in a few weeks time.

On one of his regular visits to that agency the manager had a request for him. "I wonder if you could spare a few minutes after we have our meeting, David?" she asked. "There is someone here in the office would like to speak to you."

"That will not be a problem," David replied, for in the course of his work he had to be prepared to attempt to untangle all kinds of situations. These were usually social or emotional, but seldom spiritual.

Thus it was that David was introduced to Denise and they were left to talk. Perhaps it would be more correct to say that Denise did most of the talking with David assuming the role of sympathetic and understanding listener.

The story she had to tell was one that was painfully familiar to David and Helen. The fears and anxieties she expressed were no different from theirs of a few years back.

When Denise had poured out her heart to him, David gave her some practical advice, one element of which was to contact Teen Challenge and ask if they would have a place for her brother. He also told her of the book which was due out shortly and she was one of the first to place an order for a signed copy of it.

Little did either of them realise at the time but their meeting was not by chance. It had been ordained and ordered by God. He had used the experiences David described to encourage someone, allowing them to see a chink of hope in a bleak predicament, weeks before the book had ever rolled off the presses!

Denise duly received her signed copy following the book launch, and like many others read it through at one sitting. She was amazed at the similarities between the trials which had beset the Runcie family, and those surrounding her own.

On finishing the book Denise contacted the manager of the new Teen Challenge Centre at Sunnybrae, Fyvie, Aberdeenshire. He was very understanding and helpful and explained the process involved in the centre taking in applicants.

The concerned sister asked for an application form which she in turn forwarded to her brother. The timing was right, as it always is when God is involved. Martin, her brother, was ready to seek help. Desperation was setting in and time was passing him by...

When David contacted Martin recently he wrote out his story, which is best recorded in his own words...

"I was born in Fraserburgh and brought up in the nearby village of Sandhaven. For the first nine years of my life I enjoyed a happy childhood with good parents who worked extremely hard to raise my two sisters and me. When an opportunity came up for my dad to secure a better paid job, we all moved south to a place called Irvine in Ayrshire. This was exciting but also scary at the same time.

When I was about 14 I started smoking cigarettes and before I was 16 I was hanging around with the wrong crowd and got into smoking cannabis. Throughout my teenage years and into my early twenties my life began to spiral out of control.

I was in a relationship and at the age of 23 fathered a child, a daughter called Shannon. Three years after Shannon was born I ended up in prison after I got caught in possession of a significant amount of cannabis which I was selling to fund a cocaine and temazepam addiction.

It was while I was in jail that I was introduced to heroin. I was going through a really tough time and when I saw someone taking heroin I decided to try it myself. To be honest, I thought it was great for all my worries seemed to disappear.

When I had served my sentence and was released from prison in October 1999 I quickly became a full blown heroin addict. This led to more serious problems. I nearly lost a leg and had to have an operation to cut an infected lump out of my chest after I was kicked in a fight.

Thankfully, though, while I was in hospital, my sister Denise got talking to David Runcie. Denise explained my situation and asked for his help.

He shared his own experiences in dealing with family members in the throes of drug addiction and pointed Denise in the direction of Teen Challenge, Sunnybrae, (a new centre in rural Aberdeenshire.) He also gave her a copy of the book 'Out of the Deep,' soon after it came out.

My mum and Denise wasted no time in getting me to contact Sunnybrae and I was interviewed by the centre manager, Gordon Cruden. He painted a grim picture of life there, probably to test and see how much I wanted the programme. He needn't have worried. I was so sick and tired of being sick and tired I knew I needed to do something. If I didn't I would soon be dead.

On November 17, 2003 I entered the Teen Challenge programme a broken man, physically, mentally and emotionally. Although I found it very difficult to change at first, as I couldn't get my head around Christianity, I found myself being drawn towards Jesus. I could see Him at work in the people around me – people like Matthew Runcie who was a staff member while I was a resident – and I wanted what they had.

God had begun to work in my heart and in February, 2004, I gave my life to the Lord. Since then I have been completely transformed from a lying, stealing, cheating heroin addict into a loving father, devoted husband and dedicated disciple of Christ.

I now have a full time job in Teen Challenge and have been blessed with a wonderful relationship with both my daughter Shannon, and my beautiful wife Lindsay, whom I married in August 2008.

I read the book 'Out of the Deep' while I was a resident at Sunnybrae and remember being amazed at how even within a Christian home I could relate to the troubles the family faced due to heroin addiction. I could identify with the boys because of what my own family had to put up with. Reading it gave me a tremendous sense of hope that my life would turn out OK. I am very grateful to David Runcie for taking the time to talk to my sister, to Gordon at Sunnybrae for giving me the opportunity to change my life and to my family for always supporting me.

Without God putting these people in my life at the right time I have no idea where I would have ended up.

All the glory goes to Him!"

Matthew, who was a staff member when Martin was a resident in the Teen Challenge centre at Sunnybrae, was one of the lads whose remarkable story was featured in this book. Yet he was merely one of its five major characters. It surely must be worth recounting how God has blessed the lives of David and Helen and their three sons as they have become an expanding family unit over the past nine years.

Chapter 34
# THE RUNCIE RESTORATION PROJECT

'Time and tide wait for no man,' they say, and with the Runcie family this has proved the case. There have been many happy changes since 'Out of the Deep,' was first published.

David and Helen have witnessed a continuous growth in their family circle, and what thrills them most is that they have all remained so close. Seldom a day passes but a son or daughter-in-law will call in for a chat, often with a grandchild in tow. On the rare days when no one calls at the door some family member will invariably ring up to register a significant milestone in a little one's physical or mental development or discuss a problem that has arisen.

It is pleasing to note how this has come about following a steady sequence of weddings and 'wee ones' over the years.

First of the boys to announce his engagement was Matthew. He and Ashley had been dating for some time and revealed they were planning to marry about a year later, in June 2004. That day proved such an incredible birthday present for David and Helen both of whom celebrated their fiftieth birthdays that month.

All were thankful for the bright sunny day it turned out to be with all the Christians present praising God with awed gratitude for the fact that five of the bridal party were former participants in the rehab programme at Teen Challenge.

That memorable wedding day was just the start of an exciting period of unforgettable events for the Runcies. Just before Matthew and Ashley's wedding, David the son revealed that he was getting engaged to Heather and they were planning to marry in 2005.

What a tremendous year that proved to be!

On June 23, 2005, Ashley and Matthew presented David and Helen with their first grandchild. A little girl! After all the boys they were thrilled to have a girl in the family to dote upon. During that summer Jonathan also met a young lady, and as the months passed Joanna became a 'regular' in the Runcie household.

In the autumn the family travelled to USA for the next exciting event on the calendar. This was the wedding of David junior and Heather, which was scheduled to take place in the Smoky Mountains of Tennessee. This was a small family ceremony that David the dad had the privilege of conducting. All those attending had made a long journey to be present, but that was not to be compared to the emotional and spiritual journey the family had completed up until that point. God had brought them all so far, and through so much, that their hearts were simply overflowing with joy.

There was a tremendous buzz about the household with these weddings to be arranged and attended and a little granddaughter coming and going and growing week by week. These were newly introduced activities, however, and as such were additional to David and Helen's already busy home, work and church schedule.

They were still being invited to church meetings and Christian functions to tell their story. The interest in the drama that was 'Out of the Deep,' never seemed to wane. There was a period when things were happening in and around their lives in such quick succession that there seemed to be some new development to report at every meeting in which they took part!

The Lord had 'done great things,' for them, and they were so very glad!

They simply continued to praise Him for all that was past, and trust Him for all that was to come.

There was a lot still to come, too!

June 2006 was yet another landmark month. David and Helen were just home a few days after celebrating their little granddaughter's first birthday with her, plus her mum and dad and their family friends, when Jonathan told them his good news. He had proposed to Joanna, she had accepted, and they were planning to marry a year later.

That was on June 15, 2007, and it was another bright and sunny day for yet another, a third, Runcie wedding. This was a home 'match' in the best sense of the word, with David, the dad, conducting the service for his youngest son and his bride in Bethesda Evangelical Church, Fraserburgh.

Since then David and Helen have welcomed another three grandchildren into the family circle, two girls and a boy. Their list of birthdays to remember and presents to buy quadrupled in less than two years!

David, the son, and Heather's first baby, a little girl, was born in December 2007 and then in February 2008 Matthew and Ashley presented their parents with a grandson. Following on from that, Jonathan and Joanna also became parents, giving David and Helen their third granddaughter, in June 2009.

After all the trauma and instability of the three boys' early years in employment, they are now settled in permanent jobs. David junior has followed his father into social work and is studying part-time for a university degree, Matthew works in the off-shore oil industry and Jonathan is a refrigeration engineer.

This family, once devastated by drugs has been truly

delivered and subsequently blessed by God, far above anything they could ever have asked or imagined.

What then of the future?

Their trust is still in God. It can't possibly be in anything, or anyone, else. Time has passed, circumstances have changed and the family circle has widened. Their Heavenly Father has remained unchangeable, though, proving His promise to be 'the same yesterday, today and forever.' The wonderful thing is that He hasn't yet completed His Runcie Restoration Project, either.

David and Helen, David and Heather, Matthew and Ashley, Jonathan and Joanna and all their families can say, or sing, with acute awareness and comforting assurance,

"He's still working on me
To make me what I ought to be.
It took Him just a week to make the moon and stars,
The sun and the earth and Jupiter and Mars.
How loving and patient He must be,
'Cause He's still working on me.

There really ought to be a sign upon my heart,
'Don't judge me yet, there's an unfinished part.'
But I'll be better just according to His plan
Fashioned by the Master's loving hands."

The end product will be worth seeing when God presides over the unveiling of His completed Runcie family masterpiece.

That is scheduled to take place in heaven, on a date yet to be announced.